LISTEN
DEBORAH PEZZUTO

Copyright © 2020 by Deborah Pezzuto

All rights reserved.

No part of this book may be reproduced in any form or by any electronic or mechanical means, including information storage and retrieval systems, without written permission from the author, except for the use of brief quotations in a book review.

For Papa (my babbo)
because family is what you make with love – your
blood runs through your grandchildren no matter
what, and you will never be forgotten xx

INTRODUCTION

One summer morning in 2011, Deborah Pezzuto leaves her New York apartment to give birth to her much-wanted twins. With her husband, toddler daughter, and loving Italian family behind her, she cannot wait to fulfil her dream of a family who will have the most wonderful experiences and travel the world.

But Deborah's own world is shattered when she is told that her baby boys have been born profoundly deaf. Thrown into a constant whirl of doctors, never-ending hospital appointments, and overwhelming choices, she has to reevaluate everything she has ever believed, listen to her heart, and listen to her intuition that tells her this a fight she cannot lose.

This is the remarkable story of a mother's love and her determination to do all she can to give her twins the life they deserve - a life she has to battle for, even when she feels she has nothing more to give.

As an inspirational life coach, Deborah now works with people to help them achieve their dreams, transform their lives, and challenge their false beliefs. Her story is filled with words which show how anyone can reach the life they have always wanted. Showcasing strength and determination, and a willingness to fight for what you believe in, this memoir will speak to anyone who is willing to listen.

CONTENTS

PROLOGUE 1
CHAPTER 1 3
CHAPTER 2 17
CHAPTER 3 30
CHAPTER 4 42
CHAPTER 5 55
CHAPTER 6 69
CHAPTER 7 83
CHAPTER 8 96
CHAPTER 9 109
CHAPTER 10 120
CHAPTER 11 134
CHAPTER 12 149
CHAPTER 13 165
CHAPTER 14 175
CHAPTER 15 183
CHAPTER 16 198
CHAPTER 17 215
CHAPTER 18 234
EPILOGUE 253
LETTERS TO MY CHILDREN 255
ACKNOWLEDGMENTS 260
ABOUT THE AUTHOR 264

PROLOGUE

'Ready?'

The voice of my husband broke through my daydream, sounding very far away despite him standing next to me. It was only 6am, but I had been thinking of the day ahead, of what it would bring, for such a long time.

'Deborah,' he said gently, at my side. 'It's time to go.'

Smiling at him, I hauled myself from the chair. My entire body was exhausted, heavy from top to toe, the months and months of pregnancy taking their toll but, finally, coming to an end.

'Yes, I am ready,' I told Alessandro. 'Let me just check my bag one more time.'

In amongst all of the things for me and Ale, were the newborn essentials:

Babygro – check.

Baby vest – check.

Baby hat – check.

Going home outfit – check.

And again.

Babygro – check.

Baby vest – check.

Baby hat – check.

Going home outfit – check.

Two of everything – for our twins. Our twin boys who were going to make our family so wonderful. I couldn't wait to bring home double the amount of everything. Twenty fingers and twenty toes, two button noses, everything twice over. People had been saying to me, 'twice the trouble, twice the hard work', but I was looking forward to it so much. Our life together would be such an adventure. We would travel – Alessandro and I had already done so much of that since our early years in Italy. They would see a strong mother who worked and had an exciting career, but who always had time for them. Time to love and play and enjoy them all.

I just had to get the caesarean out of the way, and then we could move on to our new reality. When we returned to our New York apartment, we would be a family of five. With our daughter, Keisha, only sixteen months old, we would have three tiny children, and I couldn't be happier at the prospect. This had been a difficult pregnancy, from conception to this point, but the thought of holding all my babies in my arms was a beautiful one – even if it would be a logistical nightmare.

They say that if you want to make God laugh, tell Him your plans, but we were pragmatic people and we had lived wonderful lives so far – what could possibly go wrong?

CHAPTER ONE
SPENSIERATA

Everyone's story has to start somewhere, and my somewhere is when I lived in Italy as a little girl. What I remember most is that I was a happy child, and no one can really ask for more than that. My life in Brindisi, on the heel of the Italian boot, was wonderful; yes, my parents were very traditional, but they loved and supported me in everything, which is all any child can hope for. My sister, Mariaclaudia, was one year older than me. She was always there as a friend to play with and, as a sporty child, I spent most of my time outside or swimming with her. In fact, my dream was to be a swimmer when I grew up and, for that, I trained every day after school, always encouraged by Mamma and Babbo. They were always so focused on us and my world was family, friends, school and sport. I was raised to be happy, to be happy-go-lucky and carefree, or *spensierata* as we say in Italy.

Most weekends, my parents would take us to a little village close to Brindisi, called Monticelli. We went to our second house in a little village at the beach, a small place where everyone knew everyone else, with beautiful houses which were white all year round. I have such good memories of life and of family from that time with the sand, the wildlife, the happiness that surrounded me. I loved that place and return even now; it showed me the value of family and of enjoying simple moments.

Looking back, I can see that my mood is like my mamma's although I look like Babbo. She was always happy and positive, whereas he was very serious. Babbo was a geriatrics doctor, so perhaps, because of his job, he was used to being like that and it just spilled over into his everyday personality. I don't know but I do know that he loved the way Mamma and I approached life as it was so different to his way. My mamma was very academic and always wanted me to study, but she also impressed upon me that travel mattered hugely.

'With travel,' she would tell me, 'you see more than places, you see people and cultures, and you see what is important. Think big, go everywhere and take on board what the world has to offer. Always do your best, Deborah; if you do that, you will be proud of yourself and you will be able to reach even higher. Never settle for less than you can achieve, and never think that there is no more for you to learn. Learn whenever and wherever you can, education is the key. There is a whole world out there – see new people, visit new places. You will never regret it.'

These were words I would remember and always try to live by, but, at that age, I could not do anything about it. I could not start to travel on my own, after all, so I concentrated on what did make me happy – which was sport. Although being active was what I really wanted to do, I was also very ill at times when I was young. For a while I was a chubby child, but photographs show that changed due to periods of bad health which had more and more of an effect as I got older. The problem began almost as soon as I was born until I was about ten years old. I suffered from a condition where there was an overload of acetone in my body. Every two months, I had a period of ten days where I could not stop vomiting. It was not dangerous - although there was a terrible smell coming from my mouth - but it was very boring to me as a child as it meant I had to stay in bed for the whole time and had to miss out on going to Monticelli. Some days I would be vomiting constantly so there was no opportunity to try and go outside to play, which seemed like the end of the world to me. These times were something I would reflect on as an adult, when I had to deal with medical issues as a parent – what I recalled from then, and what I always tried to remember, is that for the child, this is their normal. They don't know anything else in their world. Even if they see other children living different lives, they don't always apply that to themselves. If it begins when they are a baby, then they have no concept of those others anyway. By the time I had some awareness of the acetone overload which hit me every so often, I was almost accepting of it.

As my babbo was a doctor, he would sometimes give me an injection to try and stop the sickness, but those times remain a lasting memory from my childhood. He was a very caring man and hated when he saw me that way, as most parents would, and I always felt that he loved me so much it hurt him to watch. Even now, if I am ill from the flu, I panic a little as it takes me back to those days and I remember his reaction, the worry on his face. There was some confusion there for me as it was, as I have said, just normal life for me, but when I saw his concern, I did wonder whether it was something to worry about, and I think that is where my increasing worry about it came from. That taught me an important lesson – you should not let the reactions or concerns of others become your reactions or concerns. You must always try to own your feelings and responses as you cannot take responsibility for others who are reacting differently. If you can stay calm or see a route through things, it is vital that you do not let others change that. Of course, as a child, I did not have that way of interpreting things, but I can now see it was important.

As time went on, I became thinner from the toll it all took on my body and I changed from a chubby child into a very thin one. The illness was something my father did his best to tackle – not just from a medical perspective, but from that of a parent. There were many times when he would even try to do things differently if I felt it was coming on, presumably to try and change my mindset.

'Today, Deborah,' he would say, 'I will drive a different street to get us home. You'll see; that will change things. Yesterday, you did not feel well and we took the other street – maybe that way was bad for you – let us change our route and perhaps it will be better.' Of course, it wasn't, it was just superstition, but it showed that he was always thoughtful, always caring for me.

My father was the anxious parent but that did not completely transfer to me until many years later. I was emotionally secure as a child, and pragmatic as a young woman. *La spensieratezza* was in my blood, even if illness sometimes restricted me. I knew that I would have to make my way in the world, using that settled childhood as a foundation, and I would do it in the way my mother had told me. In Italy, especially in the south, opportunities come from education in a way that is completely unique. Nothing else will afford you what education brings. It is still a very church-fearing country, with centuries of Catholicism and fear for the Church infiltrating through practically every family. I wanted to break away from that.

Babbo was very clever and had been good at everything at university; not to show off, but just because he loved to learn. Mamma was a French teacher at a high school, so they were both very strict about studying. I think that my sister was more consistent at school – I was less applied to learning at that stage. I hated Latin, for example, which is seen as a very important subject in Italy. I didn't think it was important at all, but I did love English; my dream, from about the age of 14, was to go to London.

'You have to work hard at school, get the grades, then you can do the trip,' Babbo said.

Mamma was always keen on any travel I wanted to make as, from a young age, she had told me that I needed to go further than where we lived to achieve anything. The south of Italy is beautiful, but it is not a place of ambition, especially for women. You are a wife and a mother first and foremost – or at least that was the case when I was a child, living in a very conservative place.

'You want opportunity, you travel and you go north to study when you leave home,' said Mamma.

They both encouraged my independence and I was so lucky that they gave me opportunities. Both of them believed that my future was somewhere other than our tiny city.

The trip to London was something I desperately wanted. I always chose my friends carefully and valued loyalty, and I was very enthusiastic about spending more time with them, as well as visiting somewhere new. I actually think I had quite a simple personality! I hated drama and I had a lot of respect for my friends and my family. As I have grown older, that has helped me in life so much. As things became harder, I always tried to find a straight line through life, and to take the option which was right, rather than the one which anyone else might have tried to persuade me to adopt.

However, I had a disappointment waiting for me which was entirely my own fault. In Italy, in high school, if you don't reach a certain, minimum score in a subject, you have to continue to study that topic over the summer, then resit the exam in September. I had foolishly chosen three scientific subjects and, even more foolishly, did not study nearly hard enough. I had three repeats to do. Mamma was very cross, but Babbo needed to take it further, so called a meeting.

'Deborah,' he said to me with a completely serious face, 'if you do not do this properly, I will have a stroke. Is that what you want?' Although I thought it extremely unlikely, of course I did not want it! I was fine about it all myself, but it was hard to explain to the conservative people in our family that I had done so badly as this had never happened to any of my relatives before. However, I had London on my mind, and knew I had to do this. It was quite straightforward for me – I would study, I would pass. I actually think it was something of a breakthrough for my parents. They saw me make that decision and they saw me follow it through. They saw that I could do things when I wanted to, and that they didn't need to worry about me.

I did go to London and it did change me in many ways. The most obvious change to other people was that I now had brightly-coloured hair – one side pink, one side green. The fashion and style of London had really influenced me and, more than ever, I wanted to break out of my small town where everyone and everything seemed so dull. I loved the atmosphere and energy of London, the way that each person seemed to find something that was just for them – they found their music, their style, and there seemed to be a group for everyone to fit into, even the loners, the ones that didn't think they belonged anywhere. I would sit on the streets beside landmarks and on the steps of famous monuments, soaking everything in, feeling so *alive*. This was a place where opportunities were on every corner and it made me want to travel forever. Who knew what I would find in other countries, other cities? I wanted to find out.

After the first trip, Babbo came to pick me up from the airport with his friend. As I walked towards them, his friend said, 'I *think* the girl with the coloured hair is Deborah!' With my hair and my London clothes, I was not the same girl who had left – and they all laughed about how quickly I'd changed as soon as I left Brindisi. London for me had been all about David Bowie and style, music and atmosphere, and I wanted to bring all of that back with me. When I came home with four earrings in one ear, Babbo just laughed at how contrary I was compared to him. He was a man who thought he was being daringly casual if he wore a shirt with jeans! He always said that my energy gave him a lift as he suffered terribly with depression.

When I finished school, all that I knew was that, unlike many in my family, I did not want to study medicine or law; and, as Mamma had always encouraged, I needed to get away from Brindisi. So, I did exactly what she had always told me to do – I left. I went to Florence to study political science, to the

UK to learn English, to Paris to be able to speak French. Initially, I had dreams of studying in Rome, but my sister was in Florence and our parents couldn't afford for both of us to be in different places, to maintain two of us separately. So, I went to Florence where Mariaclaudia was based, to make sure there were some economies of scale. Although Babbo was a doctor, we were not rich, so two daughters in separate places, both needing some support through their education, was not an option.

Florence was an amazing place in which to study, and I was there for four years. I began to specialise in International Law halfway through my degree as I had a new ambition – I wanted to be a diplomat. Many in the diplomatic service had both studied and taught at my institution, the Cesare Alfieri Political Science University, and I was influenced by their wonderful talks and achievements. However, that soon passed as I realised I didn't really have the personality for such a career. I wanted to be part of a team, to build a group of people who I could trust, and to delegate duties because of that trust. I couldn't really see myself in a job which involved a degree of arrogance and also political manoeuvring. When I believed in something, I believed in it with all my heart – I would be incapable of backing something just because it was seen as politically useful. I may have been in the city of Machiavelli, but strategy was not for me!

Once I graduated, I moved to Milano to do a Masters in Advertising and Marketing, which led me to my MBA when I was 23 years old. Immediately after graduating, I found a position in advertising. This was very lucky as unemployment in that field is so high, even if you are willing to do it voluntarily for the experience. I did an unpaid internship for six months but the company only wanted to keep me on if I was willing to continue doing it for free. In Italy, this is quite common, but I couldn't afford to keep going with that sort of arrangement. I was 24 years old by then and spent four months looking for paying jobs. I did anything in the meantime – working in shops, surveys on the street, counting footfall, doing museum work. But then, I was very lucky to find something. I had quite a specialised area of expertise which was becoming more in demand, and I began a four year spell working with a company called Pirella, Gottsche & Lowe. This was a wonderful part of my life; I was young and enthusiastic, with the world at my feet, and I made such plans. I didn't need attention or drama, and I was very happy. This was just the sort of world I wanted to be in. I had been raised in an environment where women and men played very stereotypical roles, but also with my mother telling me to travel and experience life. In my twenties, I managed it all in this atmosphere. I was there until I was 29 then left to join another company called Mindshare WWP Group, a prestigious media group.

Sadly, not everything was perfect. I was living with a boyfriend for part of that time and discovered he was having an affair. I kicked him out of my house for cheating on me, which did take its emotional toll, but I tried to stay strong. I lost a lot of weight through the stress and often felt very low, but I knew one thing – I needed to get him out of my life. This was, however, also a difficult time in another way. Not long after we split up, I was having terrible headaches which I realised were related to a problem I had suffered from in childhood which I never really spoke about.

I had been born with a facial problem which meant that the top of my palate was smaller than the bottom, and I was on pills constantly. As a child, I always tried to make sure that my hair covered my face as I knew that I looked different, and I hated it. By the time I was 30, my headaches were becoming debilitating. I was often at doctor's appointments. One day, he told me that he knew of a specialist in Zurich who was planning to come to Milano. My own doctor believed that the headaches were being caused by the problem with my palate as even basic tasks such as eating would put a lot of effort onto my other muscles. I agreed with the surgeon from Zurich when he suggested that I undergo major facial surgery. The result was remarkable. I had huge changes under my eyes, I could move my mouth properly and, most wonderful of all, the headaches disappeared. There was no maxillo pressure at all, and even the day after the surgery I managed to eat. I had a note in my passport to say that my face looked different to the one in the photo as there had been such an amazing transformation. However, for the first fifteen days after the surgery, my face was so swollen that I covered it whenever someone looked at me. It was a big step to undergo such a procedure, so I had needed to find the courage as this was what I had truly wanted. Again, a lesson which would stay with me forever.

I think that, until that point, I had preferred not to look too deeply at how the disfigurement had affected me as a child. I did think that people were laughing at me – they didn't see me as a kind, blue eyed, blonde haired little girl; they just looked at what was wrong with me. However, oddly enough, it also helped me. I was never really anxious about illness or special needs due to my babbo being a doctor. He would brush things aside, even flu, as he had dealt with much worse through his job. I think that was very good for me, as parents who were anxious themselves would have passed that on to me. I also believe that it made me kind, and friendly. I didn't want attention because I had no wish for people to look at me, but I did want to be a good and loyal friend, to be surrounded by people I trusted and who I knew would not make fun of me. One person I always talked to about everything was Annarita, my best friend in the South of Italy – we grew up together and she is like a sister to me, and I confided in her about all of this too.

These are lessons I learned at a very young age, and they stayed with me forever. After I had the operation, those valuable traits did not disappear. I may have had a new face, but I was still Deborah. It was time for the next stage of my life to begin.

CHAPTER TWO
BECOMING ME

I was approached by the major international company Danone and asked if I would become their media manager for all of Italy. The vast majority of the job would involve working on TV ads. I jumped at the chance – a job that I really wanted with a lot of the travel I was always seeking. I loved my work and learned so much, even adding Malta to my portfolio after five years. It really was a perfect position for me. At that time, people were very loyal to brands, so there were huge opportunities through marketing to enhance and develop that loyalty. Things have changed a lot now, but back then I had the pleasure of working alongside such exciting people with fresh ideas. I felt that I'd already achieved a great deal in my life and looked forward to seeing where the future would take me. I had no idea that there was so much more ahead of me - I was 35 at the time, and the biggest change of my life so far was yet to materialise.

New people were always coming in as part of new projects or collaborations but, one day, someone arrived who was going to change my life.

Alessandro.

From the moment I met him, I liked the way he was as a person and a personality. Alessandro was out of the ordinary in my eyes, five years younger than me but so mature in his outlook, in knowing what mattered and what did not. He'd had depression when he was 21, and I was very impressed by how open he was about it and how he had used it to make life choices that were incredibly positive. He spoke constantly of how he wanted to travel, and the fact that he could speak four languages made me think he would be a wonderful companion if I managed to fulfil my dream of continuing to visit many other places too.

Alessandro worked in marketing and I was, by now, more on the advertising side of things, but a new campaign meant that we were going to be working together. He was part of a very nice group. We all went out together after work, and I started to notice him more and more. He was tall, handsome and funny, but a deep thinker. He was clearly very ambitious, like me, which was not an issue as neither of us had responsibilities. We could just make wonderful plans for our futures. It was just a friendship to begin with; I could not believe how similar he was to me and how quickly we became good friends. The first summer we met, a group of us went to India – me, Alessandro, and five other guys. I was the only woman in the gang, but I never felt uncomfortable – we were all just desperate to travel and see the world as quickly as we could. It was only after India that I started to feel more for Alessandro.

One night, we went to the cinema, just the two of us, and I think it was at that moment we looked at each other in the same way. There was a feeling that we wanted to be together, and the attraction was there. Our friendship developed into the inevitable, but still remained casual. We would spend moments with each other when we could, when we wanted to, without ever making demands on each other that felt restrictive. The passion for travel was still there and we made lots of plans to go places together, but there were things which niggled at me, which caused me to question whether this was right.

Alessandro had been in a long-term relationship and suffered in that, so I wondered whether he was ready for another attempt. The relationship I had come out of most recently had not been a healthy one either, so we were both emotionally fragile. I wanted to be sure of my feelings this time, and I did not want to be in love with someone who did not love me or take care of me. I was happy to go slow and just talk about travel rather than emotional life plans, so we would walk and talk about everything, including previous partners.

I don't know what changed, but something did. In 2006, we started what I thought of as a real relationship but I began to question how we were. I wanted more, I wanted to know where we stood, and whether Alessandro saw any future with me. It affected my work and I lost confidence talking in meetings if he was there. On occasions where he had to approve things, the lines were too blurred. I started to become quite scared of working in the same company as him, which wasn't my character at all. We had a double life; our professional life, and what went on when we were not in the office. I loathed bringing things up. I wasn't me, I was lost in the middle of a relationship which had seemed so good, so easy, but was now something which caused me pain.

I started looking elsewhere for a job because, as well as the conflict I felt with Alessandro as a lover and work colleague, I just didn't feel comfortable working in the same company. I had an interview with a Dutch bank who needed a media director and was delighted when they offered the post to me. They were based in Milano, but I also travelled to the Netherlands a lot. My new boss, Sergio, was so supportive with a real passion to have me there, which made me feel extremely valued, professionally. Alessandro understood why I had moved, and our relationship got better. I was so happy in my new job working with a fantastic team under a great boss. I also had my own friends, not just people who knew both of us, and I loved that. At that point, I was much more relaxed and felt I had my independence back; I was not second-guessing everything, I was not thinking of how our relationship would be all of the time. However, even although Alessandro and I pretty much lived together, it wasn't 'official'. It was easier, all of our friends knew, but he still wasn't telling me that he was committed, although we were a couple on pretty much every level.

In 2007, I finally said to him, 'Ale, what do you plan for us? Do you have a commitment to me?' Still, he wouldn't say. 'OK,' I told him, 'call me when you decide.' He wrote to me a lot during the next six months, but I did not move in my feeling that this wasn't what I needed – I wanted him, but not in this way. Then one day, he wrote, *Deborah, I have an opportunity to go to New York. I want you to come with me.*

It was to work on another aspect of the Danone company's portfolio and perhaps it would have been just what I wanted while I also worked at Danone and felt lost in our very casual relationship, but things had changed. A big part of me still wanted it, but my friends told me it would be a crazy move.

'You're not married,' they told me. 'You would be giving up everything for him, and if it ends you would be left alone, in a city on the other side of the world.'

They were right. It was still too informal, too relaxed. Plus I knew that I wanted a family. I was now 40 years old, and fast approaching a point when it would be now or never for me to have a child.

'I cannot do it,' I told Alessandro. 'I can't just give up everything in the hope that, one day, it will all be settled. I need more than that. We have spent so long not committing to each other – well, it is time. I don't know if you want what I want from life. I want a family, I want to know that I have everything at home as well as in my career.' This wasn't a Hollywood film, this was real life and people have consequences to think of, choices to consider.

'What do you want me to do? What do you want us to do, right now, at this moment?' he asked.

'I want a family,' I told him, honestly. 'I want a family and if that is not what you want too, then I can't see any future for us. Go – and only call me if you decide that we want the same things because I am not a teenager anymore. I am not a young girl with nonsense in her head. I need to know that my future is the future I want for myself.'

Alessandro did go and he wrote to me for three months, but I never replied. I had something else on my mind at that time too - strength comes from you for sure on so many levels and with so many things, and I had learned that from another terrible event in my life. In 2007, I lost my babbo during heart surgery in Milano. He had been through three bypasses and needed to have a valve changed; a procedure which was much less onerous than any bypass. He went into surgery and we never saw him again as himself. He died three days after the operation and, in my mind, they had killed him.

My mamma and sister were destroyed; I needed to act alone, I needed to be strong. Afterwards, I wrote to the doctor to ask some questions as the hospital refused to show me the documentation. We engaged a lawyer and it took two full years to get the files when a judge finally commanded it. There had indeed been a fatal mistake and it had killed my babbo. Anyone can make a mistake, doctors are only human, but I strongly believe that you shouldn't hide if you do make a mistake. That is exactly what these people did. I loved my father and he never saw my future, which breaks my heart.

I was going from Milano to south Italy every weekend because my mother needed me. She was lost when he died, she had such a fear of change. I kept going to the cemetery to see my babbo and I would talk to him; I sensed so clearly that this was the point at which I needed to develop my strength, to see how solid you have to be when something terrible happens.

With Alessandro, I had to take the same approach and leave it alone so that he could see if he wanted the same things. Then, one day, he told me he was coming back. We met as soon as he arrived in Milano and that night, at dinner, all of the stress and worry of those past three months melted away.

'I want a family, I want my future to be with you,' he whispered.

All I could say was, 'I trust you, Alessandro. I trust us – we will make a beautiful family together. This will work.'

There were many questions I had to ask myself at this point, but the main one was: when a relationship is 'almost' right but you need to change something to make it perfect, what should you do? How do you change the things that need to be changed to make it something you are entirely comfortable with? I had to be very honest with myself and accept that I was responsible for this situation. The story was going in a way that I didn't like, but I couldn't say 'stop.' I was in love with Alessandro and I didn't want to lose him, but the reality is that saying 'stop' doesn't necessarily end things, it just lets you show who you really are and what you really want. To get the relationship you want, you have to tell the truth. If you want a family, don't cheerfully say that you are fine with an open or free relationship. If you don't want a family, be honest about that too.

It matters that you are assertive – for women, that can be an issue. When women are described in that way, it has negative connotations. It is the same with words such as ambitious or self-confident. These descriptions carry subtle criticism, implying that such attributes are not right for women. For men, they are seen as positive adjectives, but we need to reclaim them, to say that we are proud to be assertive women and to take control of our own futures, that we will raise our daughters to have the same values. As part of this, I feel I shouldn't really complain about Alessandro's actions in our relationship – I had no control over how he was, I could only show who I was and what I wanted. Once you are clear about all of that, if the other person doesn't see things in the same way, give up. Never force someone to love you, never try to keep them against their better judgement (or yours). You'll lose nothing if they go, because what you had with them was built on a false version of you anyway. Would it be better for them to stay, but for you to never get your dream of what your life should be? For me, I would never have given up my dream of a family just to keep someone who had made that part of our emotional contract. I did love Alessandro and I didn't want him to go, but I knew that I would hate living a lie even more.

I think that is the right approach no matter what age you are. Since I was young, my boyfriends had actually all been wrong for me; they were cool, they didn't want a serious relationship, but I did the wrong thing . . . I chased them. I tried to become what they wanted, and I wasn't prepared to do that any longer. I used to cry when those boys were with other girls, never seeing that my responsibility was to look at my contribution to bad relationships. I needed to ask what *my* responsibilities were, not theirs. I needed to find someone who wanted the life I wanted too, and Alessandro was the culmination of all those lessons. There was no point playing games, the only thing that mattered was to be myself. If the person you are with doesn't like who you are, then they are not right for you. It wasn't that I wanted to lose him – it was the opposite. I wanted it to be perfect so we could build our life together. We needed a strong foundation and that was what I was trying to move towards when I told him what I needed from life. The fact he wanted that too, and that I had been honest about who I was, meant the world to me.

I said to my boss that I needed to be with the man I loved, and could I work at home for the company for one year? I didn't want to get married at that point and I didn't want to risk my whole life, my whole career, on something that could be lost if we were not compatible long-term. It felt right but perhaps Alessandro had changed during his time away, perhaps there was now some distance between us emotionally rather than geographically. I liked to act, but I had to be cautious too.

Two months later, I arrived in New York. I loved it. I loved how busy it was, how people were living their dreams. Yes, there were people who had not been so lucky, and there were people who felt that life was not on their side at that moment, but I had to focus on the fact that I was doing what I could do. I had been there once before, when I was 30, and the energy, the people, the sense of *life*, was something I adored. I had spent that time going to the shops in Soho and West Village, looking at all the vintage clothes, and to Times Square to see the lights. I adored the diversity and the noise. You never feel alone in New York. You are in the middle of the world. Everyone is so busy, it is all incredibly fast, but they are really friendly when you talk to them. There are so many Italian-Americans that I could often speak in my own language and feel that connection. I actually felt at home there – I still do.

When I arrived to be with Alessandro, it felt right. Life was nice, I was carefree, working from home, and all my concerns about him and feeling that our relationship had been weakened came to nothing. I loved my time with Ale and believed that he was truly the right man for me. This was a magical place, so far from Brindisi – not just in miles, but in attitude and possibilities. We had so many friends in New York and spent many evenings at (or hosting) dinner parties, enjoying nights out, trying new restaurants. Spring and summer there were amazingly beautiful, and I have many happy memories of reading books in Central Park. I loved it at Christmas too – the cold was exhilarating but perishing too! We were always busy, with Grand Central Station being one of our favourite places. Ale and I lived in a building just in front of it and adored this wonderful centre of activity. The clock in the middle is a meeting point for many people in Manhattan, surrounded by shops which sell everything. I would meet friends in a café or pick up treats for dinner, just absorbing such an incredible place.

I would dream of having children in New York and extending my life there. I would do all of the same things – and more – but there would be little people following me around, holding my hand, taking it all in. Manhattan is just the epicentre of real life. You can have and do anything there, and I was so sure we could be part of that for as long as we wanted. This was a place where anything and everything seemed possible, and I would grab every chance at every opportunity. Alessandro was by my side and we loved each other so much. We had a dream together and we would make this work. We would make everything work.

CHAPTER THREE
CATCHING DREAMS

After five years together, we decided it was time to build our family. Our dream was to adopt. Maybe this was impossible, as we were Italians living in America, but we had ten-year visas and it was worth looking into. We had demanding jobs that we worked at all day for crazy hours, then we spent any spare time looking into the process, finding the best place for adoption. I told no one as they would all have had an opinion, they would all have told us it wouldn't work, but we knew it could. I was trying to get pregnant too, but we felt it would actually be better to adopt first. I didn't know if I would be able to get pregnant at my age, especially as I had never had a child before, and we also thought there would be less chance of the adoption agencies looking on us favourably if we were expecting a child, or already had a baby. So, adoption seemed the best, right, first option.

In Italy, the adoption process is a very lengthy one – we would have had no hope of success there; our age would have disqualified us immediately. In America, this was not a problem. There was one issue which I thought might cause a problem though; while Alessandro had a visa to work, I was on one only as his partner. I knew that I would have to leave my job and look for another one if I wanted to remain in the USA. After I resigned, Danone offered me a part-time job just for a short period, and I was very happy with this. I felt alive again – once more, I was surrounded by people who understood the world of work and who afforded me interaction and engagement. I felt myself again and it was glorious to have this sense of life in the best city in the world.

The temptation was to Google every day – every adoption agency, every process, all of the pitfalls, everything to avoid, everything to prepare for, but being in New York with so many things to do, and this wonderful sense of finding myself again, meant that I could always find distractions. If I hadn't, the days would have been never-ending with research and factfinding. I needed to find the best place. I needed to give us, and the child we would love, the best chance. We had so much love to give and a child would have a wonderful life with us. It would cost a fortune, but it would be worth it to find the right way to go about things. A non-profit agency in Harlem seemed ideal, so we registered with them, starting the process to see if they, and any biological mother, would accept us. They had to be sure the child would be the priority and it would be best option for them.

'We are foreigners,' we admitted to them. 'We are Italian, but have ten-year visas and will do anything you ask to make sure this happens.'

'You can only do domestic adoption,' we were told. 'There are so many children here who need families that we have to prioritise them.' It was not an issue for us – we wanted it to be this way. In many countries, there is only closed adoption and we felt that, with such an approach, you lose the family story, which is so vital to the child. Adopting from abroad was often seen as the only thing to do. We discovered that in the USA there were so many children who were there for adoption, but they were being ignored because of the assumptions often made. Our position was that it didn't matter where the child was from, what mattered was them as a person – we wanted a child, we wanted a family, it was as simple as that. There were so many local children who needed someone to love them. The other aspect of adopting that way was that there was no history for international adoption. In fact, there was often no link to the parents at all. With domestic adoption, it was always there, and that was something we wanted to have. When we compared the situation to Italy, it was worth it. I have to say that, in fact, open adoption is seen as not good in many countries because some people are scared to have contact with birth families, scared to open their life if there is a potential risk of losing their kids. To me, that isn't the case – the relationship with the birth family gives the child a clearer future without gaps in their life.

The agency didn't make any requests for us to be married – Italian agencies would have, and they would also probably have expected it – and it was not something we had really discussed. However, one night, as we lay in bed, Alessandro turned to me and said, 'Deborah, a French friend of mine told me something interesting. He said that he just went to City Hall one day and got married.'

'Oh?' I replied. 'Just like that?'

'Yes, just like that. You know, if you want, we could check that out. Tomorrow,' he added casually.

'OK, we can go, let's do that!' And, indeed, *just like that,* we decided to get married.

The clerk at City Hall said it was easy.

'Sure – if you've got twenty bucks, you can do it,' we were told.

We booked the date we wanted online and started to prepare, but there wasn't much to do. I wasn't desperate for a big, flouncy, white dress and a demure veil. I loved vintage clothes, so I went to Brooklyn and bought a pink cocktail dress for five dollars. A pair of retro shoes made up my outfit and, on the day, a florist who was downstairs from our Manhattan apartment made me a beautiful white bouquet. Again, it was so different from Italy where you would spend at least thirty thousand euro on a wedding, inviting lots of people you barely knew (some you didn't know at all) and making a huge fuss. We didn't really think of the reactions of other people, we just hoped they would be happy for us – which they were. They knew that we didn't much care for traditional things and that we would rather spend the money on travelling.

Our wedding in 2008 at City Hall in New York was amazing for me because it was just what I wanted. It was simple and all about our love for each other. It was perfect. We went in the morning, without even telling our parents what was happening, and stood in line with so many other couples. That might make it sound like a conveyor belt, but it really wasn't. Everyone was happy and we all chatted, swapping our stories and really feeling that this was a fabulous thing to do. We had a friend for our witness and all three of us were called into a room where a judge sat under the American flag.

Once the ceremony had been concluded, she said, 'OK – time to exchange the rings.'

I looked at Alessandro.

'The rings!' I gasped. 'We forgot to bring rings!'

It was all so funny, not a moment of worry touched the whole day, and I hoped it would be a symbol of our lives together. Carefree and happy, secure in our love, ready to make a family, hopeful to travel the world. When we went to the next desk to get all of our documents, we were asked what number marriage this was for each of us. 'Our first and last,' we replied. I loved the way we married, and with the money we saved by not having a traditional Italian ceremony, a trip to Hawaii was planned. While there, we spoke of our hope for the adoption to happen. It was the main topic of conversation and we knew that the next stage was for us to write 'the book'.

The open adoption system in America works through all prospective adoptive parents writing a submission about themselves, their lives, and what the child will experience as part of their family. It felt like an audition. You need to get references and you need to jump through many hoops.

We were allocated a social worker called Linda who explained everything to us. Before we wrote what I thought of as our audition piece, we also went to a meeting with lots of other prospective parents where everyone talked of their hopes and dreams – and their concerns. I met a wonderful woman called Claire, who became my best friend in the US. She was such a support to me then, and in the years to come.

Linda confirmed that, because we were Italian, we could only apply for a domestic adoption. She asked a million questions. It is an intrusive and intensive process where even the FBI do checks - you give fingerprints and everything. The truth is, the agency and the biological mother are giving the prospective family a child, and they need to be sure.

Alessandro and I started to create an album about us - our story and passions, pictures of us as children and together. We were open to either sex, any ethnicity, anything at all; we just wanted a child to love. Linda kept coming back with more suggestions about what we could put in the album.

'It has to be honest,' she told us. 'It has to be the best way of making birth mothers think you will be the right family, the best home for the child she is carrying. You have to be very honest about who you are.' We agonised over what we put in the album at the start, thinking that we had to get it right the first time – in the event, Linda only approved it after six months!

The birth mothers registered with the agency were from all over the USA, even Alaska. We did not have a specific region of interest, we just wanted someone to want us, and for it all to go smoothly.

'How long will it take? When will it be time to meet someone? When will someone choose us, do you think?' I asked Linda, so many times. She always answered, 'We don't know.'

When the wait begins, you have hope and fear. Sometimes one takes over from the other but usually they are both there, waiting inside the wait. You make deals with yourself, silly deals, ridiculous bargains where you trade things in your mind for getting what you desperately want. There are moments, days sometimes, when you think that perhaps it is all there, within your grasp. Perhaps someone is looking at the story of your life now, perhaps they are thinking you are perfect. Perhaps they are saying that they want you, they want *you*. Then, other times, the fear creeps in. How could you possibly think this would work? Why is no one calling? Why has no one chosen you? It must be because this was a ridiculous pipedream. Everyone else has better albums. Everyone else has better pictures. There will be no child for you. Those times of darkness, however, are always driven out by the light. I started to see that while we waited, and it has stayed with me. The darkness always lifts, the light always comes.

It is when we are in the deepest trenches of negativity that positive thinking shows how much stronger it is. Not only did I see that light drives away darkness, that hope has stronger weapons than fear, I saw that love wins. Alessandro and I were stronger than ever. We desperately wanted to be parents and neither of us felt bound by any sort of need to be biologically connected to our child. We would do that through love, not genetics.

I think, when you are in the middle of something like that, you have to just go with it, take every day as it comes. We had scans and we had blood tests, we had checks and we had investigations all to get through the adoption process. Of course, with it being America, everything cost money. The fee was astronomical, but you actually get pretty much all of it back through tax breaks to thank you for adopting American children. During all of this time, I was still trying to get pregnant too, but, more than ever, we actually wanted to adopt first. We still thought it unlikely we would be seriously considered as an adoptive family if we had a small baby. The other way around would be absolutely fine. Still, at my age, I did not want to risk losing any chance, so we certainly did nothing that would prevent a pregnancy if it were to happen. In my mind, I felt no pressure about not getting pregnant as my attention was all wrapped up in the adoption process.

Adoption was our absolute priority – if I had got pregnant that would have been wonderful too, and we always had this concern that adoption might not be successful, but the truth was that an adopted child was our dream at that point. If you have always wanted a family and you need help to build it, it can seem unsurmountable. How do you do it? Where do you find the strength? The answer is that the strength is inside you. When you have a passion for something – and my passion was to be a mother – then that is what gives you strength. This time in my life was tough, but I was driven to have a family and if you have that sort of drive, you can surmount anything. If you want something so badly, you have to be committed. If you are told you cannot have a child, don't stop at that point. There must be a reason why you can't, and there must be other routes you can try. There is always a reason to look at other options, and I believe that opening up those options can give you a whole new perspective on life.

I knew from the start that having a genetic connection to any child I would mother was of absolutely no consequence to me. The things I wanted to do – to love and to care for the little one, to give them opportunities and encourage them to be all they could be – had nothing to do with whether I had conceived them. This wasn't contradictory to the fact that I was still trying to get pregnant, it just meant that I was practical. Who knew what my body could or would achieve? I certainly didn't, so it made complete sense to look at the bigger picture.

We were on the website as a 'waiting family' and, with every ring of the phone, our hopes were raised. No matter who called, our stomachs always lurched as we thought it might be the agency. We were seriously considered on one occasion when we were offered twin boys, who were six months old. However, the birth mother pulled out of the process and we were back to the beginning again. They were twin boys and the mother was foreign – the father did not want to have any responsibility and she did not feel able to take care of them alone. It really was a shock when she chose us because we would move from zero to two kids. After a few months, she withdrew but Linda told us that happened quite often and not to be worried. However, we were launched back into silence again.

'Alessandro, will we ever be chosen and will we ever be given the child who is right for our family?' I asked him one night.

'We will,' he assured me, 'as long as we keep trying.'

I knew he was right as that was what I believed 99% of the time too, but it is only natural to sometimes feel a little sorry for yourself, especially when you have such a dream of what you want your life to be. We could do this together, we could hang on until it all worked out, but I was so impatient to become a mamma, and I could not wait to give a child a wonderful life.

And then a miracle happened.

We were chosen.

CHAPTER FOUR
KEISHA

Five months after the album was completed, we were exhausted, mentally and emotionally. Every day, we wondered if we would receive *the* call. Would it be today? How long until our next dream began? It was a very draining way to live, so we decided to take some time to refresh ourselves and go to Miami for the weekend.

We hoped that a break for a few days would give us some breathing space as waiting for 'that' call was so exhausting. We felt as if we were constantly on high alert, that we couldn't settle or even dare to breathe sometimes, we were just waiting, always waiting. Then, on the 15th of March 2010, while we were in Miami, the phone did ring. It was Linda, the social worker.

'Hello Deborah,' she said, 'I have news for you.' My heart felt as if it would leap out of my chest. Was this it? Was this the moment? I could hardly bring myself to hope – but I did. We had been hoping from the start. 'There is a child without a name,' she went on. 'A little girl who is one week old. Deborah, the birth mother has chosen you and Alessandro.'

The joy I felt is something I had never experienced before. Alessandro and I danced around, the happiness pouring out of us. A little girl! A daughter! This could be it. We had been through some disappointing times on this journey, but this felt right. From the moment Linda told us about this baby, something in me just knew that she was the one.

Linda told us that a wonderful woman had decided that she wanted us for her little one. The baby was with a foster family as her birth mother had known from the start that adoption was the best choice. She already had another child, and was living with her own father, who had agreed with her decision to place the baby with another family. The little girl was in Connecticut with a lovely family who fostered another four children, but this was a temporary home for her, and Linda said that she didn't believe she would change her mind about the decision.

When you are chosen for adoption, you are not allowed to see the child for one month, as the law allows the birth mother to change her mind. It was somewhat reassuring that Linda didn't believe this would happen, but you always worry I think - there is always that little voice in your head saying *not yet; don't get too excited yet.* These are the times when you have to draw on your strength. When you are faced with moments in your life that are a crossroads, you have to be sure – you have to be sure of yourself and you have to be sure of your partner. The feeling of being at the mercy of other people's actions and their decisions was something which could have been a huge struggle. Ale and I are both pragmatic people, and if we want something we believe that it needs to be worked for, but this was a situation different to any we had come across before – we were not able to make a plan, to work out what we had to do, ourselves, to reach our goal. Yes, we had completed our album to the best of our abilities, yes, we had jumped every hurdle placed in front of us, but still, we could not simply make this happen because we had a strategy.

I believe it is at moments like this in your life that you find out who you are – and who your partner is, if you have one. It can break you, or you can learn from it. If, at the end of the day, you can honestly say that you did everything in your power to try and reach your goal, then you can put your head on your pillow that night and be proud. There was nothing we could do about the decisions and choices of others; we could only be responsible for ourselves. It is a lesson that, perhaps, some people never learn, but I feel it is one which can bring a sense of achievement. That is not to say that we did not live in a constant state of *what if?* You would have to be a robot to not have those butterflies in your tummy, the little whispers that make you wonder if your dream is about to come true, but those are natural, those are normal.

Although we had not been able to see the baby we desperately hoped would become our daughter, those rules were not in place for Linda.

I can remember her words to this day.

'She is a flower, Deborah. She has such big eyes, she watches everything – and she is waiting for you.'

It was as if everything was coming true. Those words made me feel that I could already see, in my mind, my daughter. Linda explained to us that they usually waited one month to be sure the birth family was certain regarding their decision. It was the right thing to do and we found this a very fair attitude for both sides as it would, hopefully, prevent painful moments. Linda would return to us when she was sure that the birth family was certain about things, and after the law in NY that one month must have passed.

All we had to do was wait, all we had to do was get through the month. What had worked in our favour was that the baby's birth mother had Italian blood in her from a few generations ago. We had included so many pictures of us back home, with our parents, with all of our Italian friends and family, that she felt her child would thrive in our love and care.

'She chose you because she loved your story – this made her sure,' Linda told us. 'She even wants you to name her.'

We couldn't believe it. This was clearly meant to be. This little girl with no name, was getting a step closer to joining our family. Linda gave us some more background details. The baby's mother was Caucasian and her father African-American. We took the train to the Hamptons to meet the birth mother and the grandfather, having arranged to see Linda once we got there. It was the Sunday before we were due to welcome our daughter and we were counting down the days – no, the hours, possibly the minutes! As soon as we stepped off the train, we saw Linda, and she had a broad, reassuring smile on her face. I was so very cold when I got there, which I think wasn't just due to the weather, but also the little bit of fear which was still running through me. We were so close; I did not know what I would do if this was snatched from me.

'They are here,' said Linda, 'and it's all fine. They are clear in their decision and really do want to move on.'

Relief flooded my entire body, and I know Alessandro felt the same way. We smiled at each other and could not help the happiness that we dared to dream. I had a friend who had been through this process twice, and on both occasions, the birth mother had changed her mind. It was with this renewed hope that we met them both. She was very shy and very kind, and the grandfather was very open about everything. After only ten minutes, we were all laughing together. They were so kind. They were such lovely people and it was beyond our earlier hopes that it would all work out like this. I played with the other little girl for most of the visit, and I couldn't help but wonder whether our baby would look just like her. Alessandro was very relaxed, chatting with the grandfather about Italy. Both of them told us they had chosen us from many albums and that they loved our pictures and sense of family so much, as well as the Italian links that Linda had told us they were drawn to. All they wanted was for the little girl to be loved and integrated, to be given opportunities in life, and to be cherished. Linda was African-American, so we were able to get lots of advice on making sure that this wonderful addition to our family would still retain her culture and know her roots; this was something we emphasised to everyone, and they seemed very pleased with that.

That night, when we arrived home, we were almost bouncing off the walls with happiness! It had all gone so well, and we felt that we could truly start making plans for our future as a family. Our parents and friends in Italy were thrilled. In my home country, many people who want to adopt feel it will never happen. They either have to go abroad to find a child, with all of the difficulties that entails, or they face real struggles in their home country, where they are always expected to fit narrow ideas of what makes a perfect family. When our parents found out that we were so close to bringing a baby into our family, our whole family, including them, were all ecstatic.

The next thing we needed to do was think of what to call her, as our daughter was still without a name. We checked so many lists. It wasn't that we had left it until that moment – we had checked many, many times before – but it finally felt so real at that point.

'Let's check on Google the most popular names in Harlem,' I said to Alessandro that evening. We wanted her to keep her African-American roots and culture. When we saw one in particular, we knew it was perfect.

Keisha.

The name meant happy and healthy, which was all we wanted for our wonderful baby.

The next day, I called Linda and revealed the name we loved. 'Please let her second name be something that is chosen by her birth mother and grandfather,' I asked. 'It will be a beautiful link and it will help Keisha know that they made the best choice for her.' They opted for Jayla Marie.

Keisha Jayla Marie.

A beautiful name for our little girl. I didn't feel any worry about Keisha's birth mother, and actually thought that we now had another family in New York; more links and more bonds. I didn't want to keep them away from us, they were kind, caring people.

We had bought nothing for our daughter up to that moment. Linda had advised against it in case they changed their mind. 'Just wait,' she told us. 'Wait until we all know for sure, just in case.' Now, we were panicking! Keisha was coming, and we had nothing. We went to our local department store and asked an assistant for help.

'We need everything for our baby daughter,' I told her.

'Oh, how lovely,' she replied. 'When is she due?'

'Tomorrow!' I laughed.

And there we were, frantically buying clothes, bottles, a steriliser, a cot, a buggy, everything for this little girl who would be landing into our world so soon.

We had to be at the agency the next day, at 9am sharp. We slept so little that night, so excited and full of anticipation at what was about to happen. When we arrived, my hands were shaking as I pushed the button for the elevator to arrive. We must have looked so obviously like a couple who were about to go to the room where you meet your baby as a man spoke to us without any introduction. 'Are you the parents of Keisha?' he asked.

I nodded, wondering what he was about to say.

'I just carried her here from her foster family,' he told us, smiling. 'She is beautiful, a wonderful child. You will be so happy with her.' I admit that I cried as he spoke those words, already calling us her parents, already putting us in the role we had wanted for so long. I wiped my tears away and walked into a room that seemed far too normal for what was about to happen. Immediately, Linda said everything was fine, and I let go of the breath I had been holding for what seemed like hours. I remember the red chairs. I remember thinking, *I'm going to meet my daughter.* My life, our lives, would be changed any second.

Alessandro and I did not say a word, not to anyone else, not to each other. How could we? The excitement, the curiosity of what our child would be like; how could we have chatted in the middle of that?

'We are preparing everything,' said Linda. 'Don't worry, this is just what happens. She'll be here soon.'

She went away for only a few seconds, and then, and then, and then . . .

So many people came into the room when the door finally opened. The foster family, all of Keisha's birth family - a swarm of people - but all I could see was her.

Our daughter.

The birth mother was carrying our child, our baby. I could not take my eyes from the one who would change everything. I saw her pink trousers and her pink shirt, her green pacifier, and a head full of the most beautiful dark, curly hair. She was awake and staring at everything, not crying at all, just alert and watchful. A sign of her character to come. The birth mother and I looked at each other, woman to woman, and she handed the baby to me. She was emotional, that was very clear to see, and so was I, but I felt this was something I should not show, out of respect for her and her father. I knew that she was an introverted person, but this could not have been a perfect day for her or her father. Even though they had made this decision and come to peace with it, who knows what they really felt, deep down?

'Here she is,' she said to me, her voice breaking a little. 'Here is Keisha.'

I tried to keep my own tears back, but a few dropped down my face. Relief and joy mixed together in this beautiful moment that I'd feared we might never see. In my arms, Keisha was staring up, as if to say, *Oh, you picked me up at last!* Never, not for one second, did I ever think or feel *poor Keisha*. I knew that she would have a wonderful life, and I knew that we would too, with this little girl by our side. She would be an inspiration to us. She had such a strong body, and her huge eyes never stopped staring at us, her curious look never faltering.

The foster family was so kind, staying longer than everyone else; they and their three daughters were lovely people who had helped so many kids and clearly did not do this for the money.

'Please, when you have the time, any time, can you let us know how she is getting on?' the woman said to me. 'We always think of these babies and would love to know what they become but no one ever tells us, and we aren't allowed to get in touch. She is such a special girl, and we would love to be sure that she is having a wonderful life.' I reassured them that we absolutely would send pictures and updates, as I looked at Alessandro who was now holding our daughter. Tears were falling from his eyes too as he stared at her, holding her tight as if he could not hug her closely enough.

'I need to bring you back to reality,' interrupted Linda. 'It's time for the business to begin – and you have a lot to learn!' She explained to us how to change diapers, how to dress Keisha, and how to bathe her. She went through the issues of safety you have to think of with a newborn, and when we should get in touch with a doctor if we needed to. This took an hour, and although we did, of course, pay attention, I couldn't stop myself thinking of what it would mean to be alone with our daughter. To kiss her and hug her and sing to her whenever I wanted; even being able to pick her up when I wanted seemed as if it would be a huge thing. I wanted to be able to sing her Italian songs and tell her that my father, Nonno Aldo, would always be with her. My thoughts were focused on the two constants that resonated through me, ringing with promise and the sureness of instant love.

This is the girl I will never be far from.
This is my girl for life.

I loved her in an instant, and I knew I would never stop loving her. After an hour of telling us what we needed to know, Linda asked Alessandro to get the car seat (one of our many purchases from the day before).

'Good luck!' Linda's leaving words were short but sweet, as she closed the door on our new family. Honestly, we had no idea what to do. We had never even changed a diaper before, but we had all of her words of wisdom to help us. We had called a cab and put the baby seat inside - such a normal thing to do -

and we went home, passing so many people who did not know there was a miracle driving past them.

A miracle that was our family. Many others had helped, but we had done it – we had made a family.

CHAPTER FIVE
BUILDING OUR FAMILY

It was good fortune that Alessandro's parents were staying with us, so they got to meet their granddaughter immediately. My mamma was on holiday in America at the time too, so it was just perfect. When we returned to our apartment to show Keisha off, even the doormen went crazy about her. They had known our plans and that we were going to collect her that day, and I was so touched by their enthusiasm. I have never once felt that we needed to keep the adoption process secret or act as if we should be embarrassed about all of this. I feel that openness is the best approach for all involved and felt it even more so at that point. It was lovely to have all of these people welcoming our baby, and I knew that they would be delighted to see her progress for as long as we stayed there.

The grandparents all began to cry as soon as we took her in; their joy was palpable. Keisha did nothing but stare at everyone for the first hour; she was clearly going to be a very observant and thoughtful little girl! In fact, for all of that first day, she was very serious. When we could finally bear to stop holding her and passing her round everyone who loved her, we placed her in a baby seat with music playing. Over those first few hours, we dressed her in clothes we had selected, changed her, fed her – it was all new to us, but we fell into it immediately as if this was just meant to be. At 2pm, she finally napped, her curiosity eventually being overwhelmed by sleep. Alessandro put her on his chest to nap and I felt as if my heart would burst.

She only slept for an hour, but when she finally went down for the evening, it was just the two of us. I don't think I can even describe that feeling. I sang to her in Italian and told her of my babbo, about how sad he would be not to meet her. I also felt so sad at the loss of him, but I knew that he would be so proud of her, his first granddaughter. My baby Keisha fell asleep to me telling her that she was safe, that everything would be fine, that we would give her a world of love.

'We are your mummy and daddy,' I whispered. 'I am your mamma.' With those words I felt a swell of happiness. Words that, at many points, I had wondered if I would ever say, words that I could speak to her any time I wanted. The truth – I *was* her mamma.

All of our friends and family had been waiting for the call to say that we finally had Keisha that day, and I know they were relieved and so pleased for us, but it was just her, me and Alessandro as we lay in bed later that night. Our family. We were so excited that we took hours to fall asleep, just looking at her in wonder. That was a moment of pure happiness and you don't get that often in life, when complete joy floods your body entirely.

The next day, we continued to learn all about this new little person in our lives and we also Skyped many people so that they could see her for themselves. Our home began to be full of balloons, flowers, cards, gifts – so many kind people all wanting to wish us the best of good luck. We had a great deal of responsibility to be the best parents for her as she was a gift, deserving of love and care and support forever. We had open minds and we would give our child freedom, but we also wanted to teach her whenever we could, this little girl we had wanted so much.

Ale's parents stayed for three days, and Linda came to visit after a week. We also went to a paediatrician to get Keisha checked over. 'That is the strongest girl I have ever seen,' she said, and I realised she was not the first to say those words. We had a little star in our lives! I promised to myself that I would keep her that way, I would keep her strong and I would build a strong woman. I've never gone back on that. Adoption is incredible - one day, you are two, the next day you are a family. You have no belly, and no preparation. It is just there. I was relieved that the birth mother was sure about the decision and that she wanted to move on with her life. I really had a lot of respect for her. Now, after one month, we could feel secure about Keisha because, by law, the birth parents could not change their minds. From the day we met her, the law would protect us as her parents.

In the USA, you have to stay for one year after open adoption then all of the child's documents change, but a wonderful thing was that Linda thought it was important for Keisha to have Italian links to make our family joined in as many ways as possible. So, it was arranged that we would be given a temporary American passport which allowed us to start planning a trip to Italy for a week when Keisha turned three months old. It was very trusting because, really, you could disappear! She had to get vaccinations for the trip, but it was all very straightforward. Even the way we were checked up on by the agency was changing by that point. The social worker comes to your house once a week to check that the child is clean and safe, and that there are no problems. Then, after three months, the visits change – with their blessing that we go to Italy, there would be flexibility there too.

'You know, that little girl will have a fantastic life with you. Never doubt yourselves,' Linda encouraged us.

We arrived in Italy in May and all of my relatives were there to see her. It was the most wonderful time – the sun and the sea, the happiness and the relaxed feel of everything. I really did feel like a mamma instantly, as if I had been born for the role. I was also lucky in that a very good friend of mine, Claire, had adopted a baby who was just one week older than Keisha, from the same foster family. Her child was with her only six days after ours, so it meant that we could learn together, and know that we each knew exactly how this felt. It was a lovely time, being in parks, walking with our children in their prams, and feeling that New York was a magical place where our dreams had come true. Claire was a wonderful friend and would prove that a hundred times over in the future.

I went back to work when Keisha was four months old. I loved being a mamma, but I wanted my daughter to see that women also worked, that they had dreams and a world outside the home too. I believe that everyone should be encouraged to be the best version of themselves, and I firmly believe that women benefit so much if they can feel free to have a life that is not solely based around their family responsibilities. It does not mean that you love your child less, or that you are bored when you spend time with them, it means that you value your identity and that you are teaching them the values of independence. I did not want Keisha to think that only men had careers – my own career was very important to me, and I hoped to pass a positive message to her that women can strive to achieve everything in their lives. It's not about being perfect. Life is about effort, and when you decide to implement that effort into your life - every single day - that's where transformation happens. We all need consistency, adults and children, men and women. If you always remember why you started, you will do it; you just need to keep going. I needed to get that balance in my life, between work and being a mamma, so I took my own advice. I kept going, remembering all the time that we were so lucky, and we had started this in the first place to have a family and a happy, balanced life. At this point, we also realised that there was more to add - another layer. It was time to take our dreams to another level.

We adored being a family, but we knew that we wanted to have more children. Unfortunately, that was clearly not going to happen at my age, and with my history of not being able to conceive naturally. We'd had our fertility checked before the adoption and knew that our chances of a natural conception were very low. When we got that news, I had actually tried to stimulate egg production, but it was no good. The doctor who told us that it hadn't worked was very cold. 'It's not easy at your age,' he said. 'We can never guarantee anything and your fertility has dropped so much.' I saw four women coming out with happiness on their faces while I was in that waiting room, but I was not to be one of them. I was 43 years old and had never been pregnant.

As we weren't sure that we would be in the USA long enough to go through the adoption process again, we decided to try IVF. Adopting Keisha had taken so long and perhaps now they would feel that as we already had a very young child, it wouldn't be right to add more babies to the mix. It is a strange position to be in. If you are conceiving babies naturally, then no one can judge, no one can say they are too close together or perhaps you won't be a very good parent. As soon as you enter the adoption or fertility system, that changes. You get quantified and put into boxes, every aspect of you is analysed, and suddenly every professional you see feels free to judge you. You have to just accept this as part of the process. You can't fight it formally, but you can work on your own mind and your own attitude, coming to peace with it all and realising this is simply a necessary part of getting to where you want to be.

This is a lesson for all of life. It is very rare that you can simply click your fingers and all your dreams come true. If you have something to focus on, ignore the noise. There will always be people who want to drag you down, either directly or by their negativity. Don't allow them to do that. Focusing on your dream and your plan, achieving them through hard work and application, is what matters.

Going by what I believed, and what Alessandro believed too, we decided to go for it, to try for egg stimulation and then for full IVF. Maybe it was because we are Italian and love the idea of family, but we knew that Keisha needed a sibling. What we had to find was a clinic close by our apartment and act as soon as we could – in fact, we made the decision as soon as the doctor said my FSH levels were too low and that, although we could keep trying to conceive, it wasn't very likely to succeed. IVF isn't just psychologically, physically and emotionally demanding, it can be a logistical nightmare. NYU hospital was nearest to us - a six block walk which I could get to for 7am appointments. We were quickly told that there was almost no chance that I would produce any eggs which could be used for fertilisation and implantation. This was a hurdle, but it could be overcome.

I always clung on to the things that could help – Ale's sperm was fine, as we had expected as he had undergone previous surgery in Milano to make the motility better. I was going to take fertility drugs to try and see if I could produce better eggs. We had a plan, and that always helps. I would get up 6am, shower, then walk the six blocks to the clinic by the Hudson River, always filling my mind with positive thoughts.

You are doing this for Keisha, you have to do this for Keisha, I would tell myself. When I got there, the elevator took me to the 4th floor, opening into a purple waiting room, filled with women at different stages of the process, but all like me in one form or another. You could almost feel the anxiety; all of us were there as early as possible, hoping that today's process would start as soon as it could, and we would try and have a normal day once it was over. Across the tables and on window ledges were folders about the clinic, telling everyone about the procedures and treatments – but there were no pictures of babies on the walls, which I thought was telling. They didn't want to get your hopes up I guess, to keep reminding you of what you might never have.

The other thing I remember so clearly was that this was the American system through and through. As soon as you went in, they wanted you to pay. It was such an emotionally fraught time but showing them you had the money was the main priority. Through work, Alessandro had excellent medical insurance, but each time I felt anxiety at the thought that the insurance company would maybe refuse to cover us for this procedure. I spent most of the waiting in silence, reading my book, desperate not to hear negative stories.

At 7am, the nurse would start calling people. Bloods would be taken, and I would be given a box of syringes and vials to use, to inject just under my belly button, at the same time every day. The nurses were all very kind and I got to know them quite well. The daily blood test was to check hormone levels, then from day five the vaginal scans would begin. All they wanted to know, and all we wanted to know, was were the eggs growing and how many were there? You become obsessed with this one part of you that can't even usually be seen. Inside, there is a battle between what your body would do naturally and what you are forcing it to do. It doesn't always comply. By this point, my period had been stopped so everything had been monitored, and they knew exactly when they were in a cycle that they could monitor. So, in effect, the treatment starts the month before the treatment, if that makes sense. Ovulation - or the lack of it - is monitored every day, and then you are in a strange limbo of waiting to see if something has happened, that is so normal for so many. People who have never been involved in this process often think it is just a matter of taking some Clomid; it is so much more than that and it has the potential to absorb your entire existence.

I can take myself back to that time in a flash – I almost feel as if I am in the waiting room, that it is 7am. I can envisage those women with their fear of hoping. Some of them had such dark faces and looked scared to hope. It was not a walk in the park in any way. Looking back, making the family album that might bring us a child had been something that was fun, but this was devoid of anything like that. The injections were extremely painful, twice a day, into my stomach. I preferred to do them myself, but after a while I was bruised and sore. I wouldn't say that I dreaded it, as they simply needed to be done – it was a means to an end – but they were something I was glad to get out of the way each day. You are alone so much during this process – with your own thoughts, or in a room injecting yourself. If you dwell on the negative thoughts, it would be very hard to find the strength to go through with IVF. You have to focus on why you are doing this and what the end result will, hopefully, be. I was not myself, that is how I remember it. I was not the Deborah I had been, or the Deborah I wanted to be. All of this was for our family, to give Keisha a sibling, but it was hard, there is no denying that.

I was now at the stage where they had to make sure that everything had hit that perfect moment and it was time for the egg retrieval to take place. It is done under a general anaesthetic so, once again, I had to spend more time in the clinic, once the bills had been paid, once the money had changed hands. I was put in a bed to wait for the anaesthetist to come and, by a wonderful coincidence, he was Italian! I could not have hoped for this, and it really did help to be able to speak to him in the language of my heart. He made me feel much calmer as he chatted away about so many things, including where we were from, how we had both come to be in New York, and how we were finding this crazy city. I was pretty sure that my experience was as different from his as it could possibly be.

We became close to him and also with his family as time went on, but at this point all I could think of was the procedure. The general anaesthetic was very light and the doctor could tell the number and quality of the eggs immediately. At this stage, Alessandro was outside, in a room, providing the sperm. That afternoon they put the sperm and egg together, and the next day they put the (hopefully fertilised) eggs in. They show you the pictures of what happened, and then call in a week to say how it is progressing. I worked during the day, but when I got home I lay on the bed as much as I could. Nothing they said would comfort me about whether or not it would be my fault if anything went wrong.

'If it doesn't work out,' I was told, 'it's not you, it's the quality of the eggs. You can run, climb a mountain, do anything you want, if the quality is good.'

I didn't believe them. Everything about my life became so careful - I was obsessed with salad and terrified in case I caught toxoplasmosis. It was almost a comedy really. Each time I went to the toilet, I was checking for blood - even though I wouldn't have seen blood as I wasn't having periods. My tummy was huge, bloated from all of the injections, but I still tried to work out if it was getting any bigger. Honestly, your life is on hold. You just stagger from one worry to the next – will the eggs be good enough, will the sperm be good enough, will the implantation take, will it all work out? You count the days between each stage of the procedures and can think of nothing but whether you will get pregnant, whether you are pregnant. I had to keep my eyes on the prize. I was bruised and exhausted, but I knew it would be worth it. I just had to believe.

CHAPTER SIX
OPTIONS

In the middle of this, Keisha was my sun, she was my light. She was growing into the child we had expected from the day she came to us. She was still curious, still bright-eyed, and always watching everything around her. I could not imagine life without my Keisha, and there were times when it seemed as if all the stars had aligned to ensure that she was the one who had joined us, that she was the one we had been blessed with. I think that my instant love for her also made me realise that we definitely wanted to be a bigger family. We were going through the adoption process again, but our previous experience had shown that it could take time and be full of heartache too.

After seven or ten days, it was just normal for me to count down the time, to wish every moment away. There were the blood tests, then I had to wait for a call between 7-8am for the results. The stress is huge. Actually, it's double stress because you aren't just waiting to see if it has worked, you are fully aware that if it hasn't you will have to do it all again. It is all incredibly emotionally draining – you feel desperate. The woman goes through so much with IVF. The hormones put you up one day, then they crash the next, and there is always - always - that fear of failure lurking around the corner. It is a completely unnatural situation and it does take a toll on your relationship. Alessandro realised it was hard, but it isn't the man who is going for the 7am injections, the clinic appointments, the hormonal changes. I don't think it is necessarily that the man in this situation is emotionally distant or not engaged, it is just that they can't really feel any of it at all. I wanted to scream at times.

From one round of IVF, you normally produce seven, or eight, or ten eggs which the clinic will look at to check the quality and see which are viable. Imagine the hormones throughout this time - you have been so unwell, with headaches and aches all through your body, and now comes an even bigger emotional onslaught. However, I was positive. I was trustful of the clinic and I believed that, in the USA, anything was possible. I didn't want to talk to the other women in the clinic because I had no place for negativity, I needed to believe this would work, that this would be the next step towards making our family.

When the nurse called after that round, I could tell immediately from the tone of her voice that the news was bad.

'I'm so sorry,' she said quietly. 'It didn't work.'

I was in shock at that point. The whole process had been so physically and emotionally difficult, but I had held onto what I thought was almost guaranteed – I would get pregnant. Now that had been taken away in just a few words, just one short phone call. I cried my heart out – not just because of the news, but because of the huge hormone crash which comes so soon. Your body realises there is no pregnancy, and it quickly moves out of that mode. As soon as Alessandro and I discussed it though, we knew that this was not the end of our journey.

'I will do it again,' I told him.

'Are you sure?' he asked. 'We know now that it isn't easy – do you definitely want to go through it all again?'

'Absolutely. Let's try as soon as we can.'

We only waited one month. When I went back to the clinic, I scanned that room. There were many of the same women there but there were also some missing. Had they been successful, or had they given up? Had they run out of money or emotional currency? In a way, it was a relief to see some of the same women. *It's not just me*, I thought. I also discovered other things. In that strange world, there is a camaraderie – we all wanted the same, but not all of us would find it. There were no lengthy conversations but, sometimes, friendship can just be a look; there is kindness in a glance that shows someone else knows what you are going through, because they are going through it too. In life, you can't guess what another person's life is, but in that room you can't hide; you know why you are there and why everyone else is there. There were many stories that I heard snippets of, but no one tells you everything. There were single women, women with cancer who had frozen their eggs, women who thought they had left it too late, women who were in a hurry and nature was not keeping up with them. It didn't matter; we all wanted the same thing and were going through the same process. In my mind, I still thought that in America everything works, you can have whatever you want, and I wanted this, so I just had to keep trying. New York is full of twins and triplets, there are celebrities everywhere not admitting to IVF, just pretending that of course they got pregnant at 48, at 50, at 52, and it was just luck that they had multiple babies. There were pregnant women everywhere I looked.

Despite my belief in the doctors and in America, I knew what I was in for - the quality of my eggs was not good, so I would struggle. For those two cycles, for the first and second, I felt as if gravity would be against me if I even stood up. I wanted to keep it all squeezed inside of me in the hope that it would work. Everyone gives you advice, but none of it sticks. You just want to do what you want to do, even if you believe in silly superstitions for a while. I could hardly bear to believe it would be good news when the phone rang on our second attempt, but it was! It had worked.

We were ecstatic. I could immediately see Alessandro move from anxiety to excitement. It was time to move on to the next stage. The clinic called us in for a heartbeat scan; it was early in the pregnancy but that is how they do things. It is both a comfort for the patient and confirmation for the clinic.

We looked at the screen in great anticipation. Of course, there was nothing to see . . . but there was something to hear. When the sonographer confirmed that there was a heartbeat, we were overjoyed. I think I stayed in bed for a week after that, staring at the ceiling, but also often with Keisha beside me. I would hug her and read to her, so happy that she would soon have a little brother or sister.

And then it was over.

We only had one week. The baby was gone, the pregnancy was over before it had really begun, and we were back to how we had been before. I was so disappointed. All I could think was, *here we go again*. All we had been given was an illusion of things working out before being slapped in the face with reality. You always try to have hope with infertility treatment. Indeed, people say, 'just think positive'. I think you have to be realistic. I certainly wasn't positive anymore. That was a dark time for me because it is not my natural state. I want to be happy and make plans that I am in control of, that I can see through because I have commitment and dedication to those plans. I couldn't do that here. It was out of my hands.

I also hated people saying they had a friend who adopted and the next day she was pregnant. She relaxed and it all worked out! It is not relaxation, it is science. 'If you'd just waited, you'd have your own child,' some would say. I wished people would think about the impact of their words.

In the depth of despair, I had to decide whether I could do it all again. I didn't know if I could face the prospect of failure once more. I had to pull on all of my strength to say to my husband, 'Yes, let's do this.' I went back to the clinic and, again, saw many of the same women. The younger ones were disappearing, but the older ones were still there. You could see the contrast between the struggling women and the successful ones, the difference between those who were happy and smiling was such a contrast to the others. It wasn't just that they were sad, it was as if they were drained; their faces grey and ashen. They looked like they had given up all hope even though they were trying again. I was happy for the ones who had success and I clung on to the fact that I had Keisha.

My hormones were again up and down in a ludicrous way, but I could also tell the signs of what was going on. This time – the third time – I knew that it hadn't worked at a very early stage, as soon as the hormone crash happened. If it had worked, my hormones would not go back down. This was unbearable, and it was time for some hard decisions – could I actually go through this again?

I had to speak candidly to Alessandro.

'What do you think? Truthfully?' I asked him. 'Don't think of what your heart wants here, think of what is actually happening. This is a terrible thing to go through and I do not know whether I can do it again.'

'Would you prefer to go to another clinic?' he wondered.

'No, it isn't that,' I replied. 'Everyone here is kind, but all of the patients are really just dollars to them. They never ask how I feel in myself, how I am coping. Everything is about money – you know that four hundred dollars gets you ten minutes to talk to someone; none of it is freely given. I don't know if I can continue to be some sort of machine. If it wasn't for Keisha . . .'

I let my words tail off because I was scared of what I was becoming. I was scared of what more losses or failures would do to me. I clung on to my daughter so much, she was getting me through, but she was little more than a baby. She had wisdom and she had strength, but I wanted to be there for her, to have fun and be a mamma who was not always thinking of injections and tests.

We went back to the clinic to get some feedback on what was happening, but I knew that I had no desire to try again.

'The problem is the quality of the eggs,' the OBGYN told me.

'Can I do something?'

'No,' he bluntly informed me. 'It's your age,'

'So, what can we do? I am not a machine.'

He was very frank. 'To be honest, it has failed three times. We can keep going, but how would you manage that? You could do another ten times - do you want to?'

I knew that I most certainly did *not* want to – the idea that I would just keep going on this treadmill of hope and then despair would be horrendous, and who knew what would ultimately happen? Would Keisha ever know me as the mother I wanted to be? Would Alessandro and I get through this? When would I know to stop? Would I always think that I should try one last time? When, when, when would that last time be?

All of these thoughts were going through my mind constantly, and I had made my peace with not having another child. We were still in the adoption process and we would just have to see what happened. We would make decisions about our careers when we needed to, and try to avoid second-guessing things.

But I had not accounted for how much Ale wanted this, how much he wanted Keisha to have siblings. When I saw his face and heard his words, I caved.

'One more try,' I said. 'That is all I can take, Alessandro – one last try.'

We made yet another appointment at the clinic.

'I need to know what I can do this time,' I said immediately. 'How can I make sure this works?'

'You can't. Not going the way you have been going – we have seen that it doesn't seem to be working at all. Deborah, you need to look at going about this in a different way if it is truly what you want.'

'What other options are there?' I asked.

'Egg donation,' I was told. 'That would absolutely be the best approach. The other benefit of that would be that Alessandro could be the father.'

Egg donation.

That would give us a much better chance. We went home and discussed it, and I realised just how much Alessandro wanted this, not the genetic link, but a brother or a sister for Keisha. If it had just been up to me? Honestly, I don't know if I would have kept going, but I could see that this was his dream, to have a big family, and haven't I always said that is what you need to fight for? This was him telling me what he wanted, in the way that, again, I believe people should in a relationship. It was something I could do, if I had to. I could do it for him, for his hope that Keisha would not be the only child in our home, that she would be surrounded by more children. The genetic link would always be irrelevant – the love was not. The more I thought about it, the more I was completely sure that the issue which stops many women from going down this route meant next to nothing to me. Like Alessandro, I had no need for a genetic connection to a baby. After all, there was none with Keisha and I loved her so much. I think that, perhaps, having her made me appreciate even more that there is no need for that genetic link. When you want a child in your life, you want to love them and support them, to give them a happy world for living in, and all the opportunities in the world. That doesn't come from your egg – it comes from your heart.

It was true, however, that we knew very little about what we were getting ourselves into as no one in our circle, or families, had chosen that option. Indeed, it is not even allowed in Italy. I knew of surrogacy but not donor eggs. This would not be the same as trying to increase my egg supply, this would mean having a fertilised egg implanted into me after a lot of medical intervention, including painful self-administered injections which were not going to be without side-effects, and then hoping that everything would work out. There was, of course, no guarantee that it would work, that there would be implantation, never mind a positive test and a pregnancy. We did all of the research we could but had no contacts with personal stories or hopes to cling on to. We also made the choice to tell no one as that would bring too much pressure because there *was* pressure, for both of us.

I was already 45 and I had never been pregnant – this was all I could try. We had to meet a psychologist, who was lovely, then we went home and chatted again about how, given that we had adopted Keisha, we couldn't not do this.

'What would I have to do?' I asked the doctor.

'We stop your period, but the other woman does everything else at that point.'

Again, I had to think about it. In fact, I took a month before I was completely sure, but then we had to chat with the clinic about things that I found quite odd. They asked what was important to us? Did we want the donor to have a certain colour of eyes, a certain colour of hair? It wasn't important to us; we were completely open. We were then told that they had a 'very nice girl' and that, like many other donors, she was doing this to pay college fees. I also found out that most of the older women who were exhausted ended up using donor eggs.

The process started all over again. 'Keisha,' I told myself. 'Do this for Keisha – she deserves a sibling.'

Did I think I would ever become pregnant? I don't know. I was 45 and I knew it was unlikely, but maybe this approach would work. I was different this time though. With the other attempts, I had been so scared to do anything; now, I wanted my life back wherever possible.

The next stage was to see whether or not the fertilised egg was looking good.

It was.

In fact, they both were.

The doctor told me there was a high risk of twins if I used both as the eggs were of very good quality, but he was also on the side of me doing that. I made the decision myself to have them both implanted, knowing that it would not necessarily work. I felt lighter and was more positive this time. The doctor had told me, 'When the egg is good, it's good. You can do whatever you want. You don't need to lie down all the time.' I did exactly what he said. After implantation, you have to stay there for two hours, but I went to the park with Keisha straight after. We did everything while we waited to hear. I was much calmer, feeling that if it works, it works.

And it did. It worked beautifully. After ten days, my hormone levels stayed up, and they found out something else from those hormone levels. Both eggs were doing well, so they suspected it might be twins indeed. I was alone when the nurse told me this and called Alessandro immediately.

'Ale! Ale! I have such news – we are waiting for twins!' I shouted. 'Two babies!' As I said it, my mind went to Keisha. 'What will this do to her life?' I asked him. 'Will she be OK?'

'Of course,' he replied, calmly. 'For Keisha this is a nice thing. She will not suffer, and we can even tell her that her siblings made their journey to our family by a different way, just as she did.'

That was a beautiful way to think of it – now all I had to do was keep my babies safe inside me for nine months, something I had never done before, but something I would now commit my life to. We did have concerns – New York is an expensive place to live, and we only had a two-bedroom apartment. We had to think about medical bills too. Alessandro had great coverage through work, but if he left that job we would be in trouble. I tried to push it all out of my mind for the moment. The most important thing was that I had finally become pregnant.

CHAPTER SEVEN
TO BE A MOTHER

We would have three children – three! In one year, we would have created a whole family and I had to focus on all the positivity within that to make sure it worked out. I had learned a great deal from my journey so far. IVF is a crazy world, something that you cannot even imagine until you are in the middle of it. You have to be positive – but also not have any illusions that this will all be easy. You have to do whatever you want so your life isn't put on hold, but accept you will have moments of being terrified that there will be bad luck. You will tell yourself that you will miscarry because you bent down for something, or went to a yoga class, when the truth is that it is all about a good egg, not what you do. The more you think, the more anxiety and pressure you put on yourself, but you mustn't underestimate the treatment or the hormonal explosion in your body.

I had been swinging between every emotion there is for so long and seen parts of me that I was shocked by – I had often lost the practical, pragmatic Deborah, and in her place came a woman who was angry one second, then lost the next. I wish I had taken every bit of support that was offered and that I hadn't acted against my natural impulses so often. I waited when that is not my character, it is contrary to who I am as I need action, I need to go after things. As soon as I started to do things, I felt more like me. I meditated and walked next to nature, finally breathing out in a way that I could never do while having all those clinic visits. There, the pressure of what I was doing and what all of those other women were doing had killed my dreams for a while. I had only told two friends - Anna and Claire - what I was going through as I didn't want negativity in my life or to feel the weight of other people's expectations, but I should have reached out more.

However, all of that was in the past. I could now focus on Keisha while I waited for the other babies. I never thought for a second that they were not my children. Your body doesn't make you a mother, the genetics don't decide that – it is what you feel for them, and how you love them; something I had known with Keshia from the moment I saw her. We didn't tell everyone our news and we never felt that it was important to explain every detail of our life to other people. I was also suffering from complete IVF exhaustion and I was sick constantly for the first trimester. Alessandro researched everything online to see what had caused it. We wondered if there was something left over in my system from the IVF, and a million other options. The truth is that many women suffer from this and there is no reason for it. It was very difficult. I had a little girl who was only fifteen months old and in desperate need of comfort and security.

Ale recalls so many times when I was in our bed, so very ill, and I would have my arms out, trying to reach her but not being able to do so as I was so weak and ill. Keisha was truly incredible - I never saw her sad, which was a miracle because what could I do? I was physically unable to move some days, many days. I had no idea that one person could be so sick, and I was desperately upset that I was missing out on being with my little girl because of this terrible hyperemesis. All I could tell myself was that there was an end point – I only had to last nine months, and surely this could not go on for that long! I focused on what we were building and the hope that soon I would be not just a mamma, but part of a whole family I had built with the man I loved.

Eventually, I had to be given intravenous fluids or I could not have coped. Keisha was so little, and Alessandro was away working a great deal, so it gave me some strength. My tiny daughter was so brave, even at that time. She'd see me lying on the floor, unable to even stand, and she would bring things to me, crawling about to get what she thought I wanted, even some of her own toys. I think that any other child would have cried to see her mamma that way, weeping and trying to hold her, unable to do so through such weakness but no, not Keisha. She always smiled.

I took her with me when I went for the IV fluids and she was always so good. Ale got the train every morning at 7am, and I would struggle out of bed and get a taxi from our apartment in Manhattan to the hospital. I always tried to laugh with her, even if it was the last thing I felt like doing, and she always smiled at me, making my heart swell with love.

I lost five kilograms in the three months of the sickness and I swear, if I had been a younger woman, I would never have even countenanced going through another pregnancy. Just like IVF, the words used to describe hyperemesis are so minimising – morning sickness does not even begin to describe what many women go through. I was always terrified it would come back, and none of the medical professionals could guarantee that it would not.

Keisha was attending a nursery at the Rockefeller Centre as I wanted her to have as normal a life as possible, and also to learn independence from a young age. After I had dropped her off, I had to make my way to hospital but I never got a taxi there. I tried to keep some normality for me too. When I picked her up, I would walk six blocks – six *big* blocks – and

I did that for the rest of the pregnancy. By the time the sickness passed, I was starting to get huge; two babies were always going to be a struggle as I was very small, but I did end up looking as if someone had inflated my belly with a balloon pump! My feet were so swollen, and I felt quite weak from carrying them both.

All of the scans were fine, and we were told that we were carrying two perfectly healthy babies.

'Would you like to know what sex they are?' the sonographer asked one day.

We didn't really want to, but it was very obvious from the scan! Our twins were boys – brothers for Keisha, sons for us. We were so excited and started to think of what we would call them. It was important to us that there was some sort of link with their big sister – she had an American name from her culture, so we decided not to call the twins anything that was Italian. After doing a lot of research, we chose Dylan and Zack. We obviously didn't know which one was which but reasoned that we would decide that when we met them. The meaning of Dylan was 'Deep Blue' and the meaning of Zack was 'Laughing Boy' – we would have to see which was which!

I was scheduled for a caesarean section at thirty-six weeks. Most twin pregnancies are dealt with like that and it was actually very lucky that I even got to that stage. Ale's parents and my mamma were staying in New York for a holiday and they planned to pick Keisha up from nursery after I had delivered. She would come in to meet her new baby brothers before anyone else.

When Ale's voice broke through my daydreams that morning and asked me if I was ready, I thought I had never been more so. It was the 25th of July 2011 and that day I would meet my sons. It was only 6am, but I had been thinking of the day ahead, thinking of what it would bring, for such a long time.

'Deborah,' he said gently, at my side. 'It's time to go.'

Smiling at him, I hauled myself from the chair. My entire body was exhausted, heavy from top to toe, the months and months of pregnancy taking their toll but, finally, coming to an end.

'Yes, I am ready,' I told Alessandro. 'Let me just check my bag one more time.'

In amongst all of the things for me and Ale, were the newborn essentials. Two of everything – for our twins. Our twin boys who were going to make our family so wonderful. I couldn't wait to bring home double the amount of everything. Twenty fingers and twenty toes, two button noses, everything twice over. People had been saying to me, 'twice the trouble, twice the hard work', but I was looking forward to it so much. Our life together would be such an adventure. We would travel – Alessandro and I had already done so much of that since our early years in Italy; we would take Keisha, Dylan and Zack on a wonderful adventure through life. They would see a strong mother, who worked and who would have an exciting career, but who always had time for them, time to love and play and enjoy them all.

I just had to get the caesarean out of the way, and then we could move on to our new reality. When we returned to our apartment, we would be a family of five. We would have three tiny children, and I couldn't be happier at the prospect. This had been a difficult pregnancy, from conception to this point, but the thought of holding all my babies in my arms was a beautiful one – even if it would be a logistical nightmare.

We got there at 6.30am, and were told the babies would be delivered, as scheduled, at 8am. I was so relieved, so tired. It had been hard, but it would be over soon. The OBGYN that day was someone I knew from earlier appointments and, like the anaesthetist, she too was of Italian origin. It was as if all of this was meant to be.

'All will be well,' she assured me. 'After the first baby is delivered, there will be around ten minutes before the next. Are you ready?'

It was all happening quickly now. After what had seemed like a very long nine months indeed, and the time before that with the pregnancies which hadn't worked out, we were going to meet our babies in no time at all. It was surreal, although in the most wonderful way. I think that with caesarean sections there is a feeling that you are almost watching everything happen, that you are slightly removed from it all, and that adds to the atmosphere.

When I was taken into the operating theatre, I was shocked by the number of staff. Each baby had his own team to check him over after delivery, which made the room seem packed with people. They always have extra staff for twin deliveries, so this was perfectly normal, but it did seem to be very busy and certainly not a quiet, darkened room where I would feel very calm. The bright lights overhead blinded me a little, but I was soon numbed for the operation, able to feel nothing from my feet to my tummy. When they asked me to wiggle my toes, I was quite sure I was doing it, but apparently not! The anaesthetic was working just fine. A green cover was placed on a frame over my belly so that I could see nothing as the section began. It is such a strange sensation; you don't feel anything, there is no pain, but it is as if there is a rattling going on inside, as if someone is washing dishes in your tummy. It is bizarre to think that you feel no discomfort, no agony when you are being cut open, but it really is true. I was simply lying there, having all of this done to me, waiting for the magical moment – or two magical moments – that would soon be here. I smiled at Alessandro and he squeezed my hand. It was happening. It was truly happening.

The first boy was born, and there was a wonderful feeling of relief when we heard him cry. This would be Dylan, the loud boy from that moment. He was screaming like crazy but that was good, that meant that everything was working. I was fine for his delivery, but I began to feel very weak soon after. I could feel my strength slip away from me and it was quite scary that it seemed to be happening so quickly. Alessandro looked so proud of his boy, but it was also clear that I was becoming very unwell, very quickly. I was told not to worry and that it would all be over soon but, when Zack was born, there was indeed another worry. He was not breathing well at all and the doctors placed a mask over him immediately. Thankfully, this was quickly resolved, and the boys were soon cleaned and clothed. I couldn't move from weakness, but Alessandro was bursting with pride as he held our babies. Although I didn't have the strength to hold them too, I was deliriously happy.

When the nurse told me they had failed their hearing test, I accepted that they were the experts – they knew what they were doing, and they would go back and check again. All I could think of was that wonderful moment when they both came out of the womb and I could hear two distinct hearts, beating very fast. I could have listened to them forever. It was incredible really. After all the IVF I had been through, I now had double! We had gone from none to a gang so quickly.

Alessandro went outside to phone our parents and tell them all was well. After I was closed up and given lots of painkillers, I did start to feel better, so was taken to a recovery room where, at last, I held my babies in my arms. It was an incredible moment. It had been such a journey to get here but now they were mine, they were the final pieces in our family jigsaw and so, so precious. I could not wait to show them to Keisha, to let her see her brothers and start to plan our lives together. I did not feel pain, I did not feel weak, I felt like a woman who had fought for her dream and who was now ready to make a wonderful world with the people I adored. I had no doubt about any of this – our battles were behind us.

Keisha's grandparents picked her up from nursery and she was soon there to take her place as the big sister. She wanted to hug them immediately. They were fast asleep and so little, much smaller than I had expected. After delivery, in the recovery room, all five of us were together as my body rested from the caesarean section. I was in pain, but triumphant.

'We've done it!' I said to Ale. 'Finally, we've done it!'

This was the culmination of our dream to be a family. The adoption, the IVF, the difficult pregnancy – none of it mattered. This was a time of celebration.

While Keisha was looking at her new siblings, the nurse brought their first bottles.

'I would like Keisha to do this,' I said. 'Are you ready to be a big sister?' She did it! She took one boy and held the bottle to his mouth as he sucked greedily. We have a picture of that, and it speaks to me that she has a wisdom that is in her very bones. It also reminds me of that brief time when we thought all was perfect.

Once they were both fed, we all hugged, and she was so excited with all that was happening. There was no jealousy, there was no crying.

I felt as if all my dreams had come true.

The babies were taken away for various tests later on that day, and the nurse soon brought them back. There are lots of tests that are conducted when a baby is born; naturally, there are twice as many with twins. There is such relief when these little people finally appear, when all ten toes and fingers are counted, when they take their first breaths, when they cry for the first time.

We had no idea.

No idea that something could be hidden.

'They're absolutely perfect,' the nurse said, as we took them in our arms again. 'They didn't pass their hearing test but that's completely understandable; sometimes, with a c-section, they get liquid in their ears and it takes a little while to come out. We'll repeat the test tomorrow, but I doubt there is a problem.'

We didn't worry at all, in fact, we didn't give it another thought. This was normal, they saw it a lot after caesareans and they were the experts. Everything was absolutely fine.

That night, Alessandro sat on a rocking chair beside me and it was perfect. We were exhausted but could not help but talk of our dreams. We planned to go to Italy the next month to present the boys and have a celebration party – that felt right. This *was* the time to celebrate; we had created a big family just because we believed in it.

They went to the nursery on their first night as new parents are encouraged to take the chance to rest – 'Once you get home, there will be none of that', we were told, 'so make the best of it!' Alessandro and I continued to talk and plan for hours. The pain was creeping through – and was much worse than I had thought – but it did not matter. We were so happy, so secure in what we had made.

Keisha, Dylan and Zack.

They were our world, and we were truly blessed.

CHAPTER EIGHT
PUNISHED

We were still so happy for those hours after their birth and into the next day. By lunchtime, friends were coming to visit, even the IVF doctor and his wife. This was a huge success for the clinic – a 45-year-old woman who had successfully given birth to two healthy boys under their care. Everyone told us not to worry about the hearing test and I honestly tried not to, until that afternoon.

As the tests began, I just had this feeling that they were not going to go well. Call it mother's intuition if you like, but there was a fear in the pit of my stomach that we were about to hear bad news. I was right. When we found out, it wasn't a big deal. It was presented in quite a casual way, and the cold fear which washed over me again was dismissed by medics.

'They've failed their hearing test again,' we were told. 'It's nothing to worry about though – there is probably just some amniotic fluid in the canal.'

And maybe, just maybe, there was a little bit of hope there for me as they *were* twins, so what was the chance really that they would both have the same problem? However, a warning light flickered at that moment. A voice whispered to me, *this is something*.

We had thought that if it was fluid from the section, it would have gone by now. We had been told that the day before. That it hadn't was a worry for me. I flitted between anxiety and optimism the whole time. They said they would do it again, and again my boys failed. Still, the medics said, 'Don't worry, don't worry,' but how could I not? In my darkest moments, my mind was racing ahead, but in my calmer ones, I went back to the thought that it was highly unlikely for non-identical twins to both have a problem. The chances were surely very low indeed.

Before I was discharged, we were told to come back in two weeks for another test. This additional test – an ABR, or auditory brainstem reaction – seemed scary. That it had such an imposing name worried me, the fact that the twins had failed so many times worried me, everything worried me. A day, an hour, a minute can change everything, and it had. I was not going home happy. Knowing there was a problem, I was devastated. The test was always in the back of my mind. When the boys were a week old, we went to see a paediatrician. I thought that Zack's forehead did not look quite right; the skull seemed awkward to me and the wrong dimensions. We were told it was fine, but I was always looking for signs. Alessandro was permanently online and found all the worst outcomes once the seed was planted. He was there for the first week after the births, and we did speak of it, we did wonder to each other as well as to ourselves whether this was something bigger. Sometimes, he would try to find a glimmer of positivity, but there was never much. At one point, I called a paediatrician in Italy, a friend of the family, who told me that he didn't think this was even possible, not with non-identical twins. 'It is so rare that it cannot be,' he said. 'Enjoy your kids.' I tried to be practical, to not jump ahead, but when I sang to Zack and Dylan, when I chattered to them, I saw no response and that built my fear. Alessandro had to go back to work after one week, so I was in New York with all three of my children, worrying about all three. Would the twins pass this test? Was I giving enough time to Keisha? My days were relentless. I was caring for two newborns, having to get Keisha to and from nursery, and also recover from the caesarean. I had someone helping at home - a woman from the Dominican Republic - but I was always exhausted and without Alessandro there what could I do?

The tests would be done in an audiometric cabin, and I arrived with Ale's parents as he was at work that day. I entered, knowing nothing of deafness, full of fear and a tiny bit of hope.

Dylan was first.

I held Zack, motionless with my baby in my arms. Struck silent too, hardly breathing. The first procedure was an auditory brain test, done by a senior audiologist called Terri Shaw. In that room, we had no idea she was to become such a part of our lives. She tested Dylan then passed him to me as she took Zack. I know that she smiled, but she gave me no indication of what had gone on at that point. Did I suspect? Of course I did, of course.

I held my breath as Zack was tested, then sat down to be given the results.

There was no sugar coating.

'We've discovered that the boys cannot hear anything,' said Terri. 'They are profoundly deaf. Both of them.' I didn't say anything. I heard the words, but actually felt quite unsure about what she was telling me. Quickly, Terri went on. 'Don't worry, please – there is hope. I'd like you to watch this.'

A film started to play on the screen that she turned to face in front of me. It was of a beautiful little girl with complete hearing loss but, somehow, she was talking completely clearly. This was not what I expected. My idea of a deaf child was one who signed, or if they spoke at all, did so in a way that was easily recognisable as that of someone who could not hear. This child was not like that at all. I could not identify any speech accent in her words at all, and she was communicating just like any other girl of her age.

'Can she hear nothing?' I asked Terri.

'She is deaf,' Terri said, nodding, 'but she has help – cochlear implants that allow her to hear. Zack and Dylan have sensorial loss in their inner ears, but they can be like this too.'

I felt that there was a little light. I listened to three hours of information, bombarded by stories and statistics, diagnoses and research findings.

'This is a tough day for you,' said Terri. 'Why not take a break, come back tomorrow?'

When I told people, I had to be factual. 'They cannot hear. The babies cannot hear. They are completely deaf.'

That was the start of responses that were all about denial. We heard everything from people saying they had asked someone, who knew someone else, who said that someone else told us it would work out fine. We heard that God had sent us this trial and that we were blessed. Someone said we should have had an abortion, just assuming we would have found a test in the womb and that we would have chosen not to have our sons if they were 'damaged'. Some friends wanted us to go to Lourdes. We all expect perfect babies, but life isn't like that and I felt other people just couldn't understand things which we simply had to accept.

When we went back to the hospital the next day, Terri understood. 'Many parents think we're crazy and then they come back in three years asking for the implants. The truth is, every day you delay is a day wasted.'

'So, do we get the surgery now, if we go for it?' I asked.

'Oh no!' she laughed. 'This is a long journey, and there are many stages.'

We got four opinions. Four. One after the other because this is not what you want for your child. When you are pregnant - especially when you have fought so hard to become pregnant – you visualise your child, and it is always perfect. Of course, there can be losses, I knew that very well as I had been there with previous pregnancies, but you have a dream and you hold on to that dream. When you are told, 'Sorry, no – that isn't how your life will be', it is only natural to kick against it. My babies? My perfect twins . . . not perfect after all? Naturally, you ask someone else. And someone else. And someone else. What I remember is that not a single medical professional was upset by us seeking second, third, fourth opinions, and that was because they knew.

They knew they were right and that their diagnosis would be confirmed.

There were tests other than the hearing ones to be done. Genetic tests and eye tests – the latter because I was obsessed with their eyes. I was sure there was something there, something else that would be a challenge. When you are thrown into something without preparation, you are so fragile, you don't know what to hold onto. We were straight onto the treadmill and lost enjoying the moment. I remember getting Keisha when she was only one month old and there were such celebrations, but this time I had two babies in my arms and a heart full of worry.

When we told many friends and family members, some were supportive, but many tended not to believe it. Actually, maybe they did, but they certainly refused to accept it, often responding with tired clichés or outright denial.

'Doctors can be wrong,' they would say. *They're not*, I would think.

'Just have faith, just have a little hope,' they would say. *I have faith, I have hope, and I know that these babies need me to make the right choices for them,* I would tell myself.

'Your boys will hear – they'll grow out of it, you'll see!' so many people told us. *This isn't something you 'grow out of', they are profoundly deaf,* I would want to scream at them.

We had no welcome party for Zack and Dylan. Keisha grew up with joy but when you have a child with special needs it's different, and I felt it at that point, I felt it so much. She had everything pink, princess things everywhere, but they had nothing. I feel I lost that part with them because I was immediately thrown into this world of deafness, a world that seemed so overwhelming.

The next person we had an appointment with was Dr Roland. He was very nice to the boys, just saying, 'Hey guys!' to them as we went in, and he was not anxious in any way. He also struck us as someone who was just very human by telling us about his own family. I needed someone who was approachable, who was not cold towards my babies. Dr Roland was very reassuring to us as he was so relaxed about the surgery. When I asked how children so small and vulnerable could undergo cochlear implants at six months, he told us it was very routine to him; in fact, he would have to leave our meeting soon as he had one to do! He was another positive voice in our lives.

After Terri at NYU had told us what was going on, Ale became lost in his thoughts. He had missed out on many of the meetings I'd had and was less informed about the journey our boys faced. I was exhausted at every call - my mum, his parents, my sister all wanted to know what was happening, but I didn't want to repeat everything word for word, so I probably told him less, which I do regret. By the time Dr Roland came along, things were slightly better as we both loved his way and his attitude.

In the last week of August, my sister Mariaclaudia phoned, full of excitement.

'You have to call someone,' she said, speaking quickly. 'In Italy, there is a girl who got the cochlear 20 years ago. I have her number for you and I am sure it will help!'

I was so excited at the prospect of talking to another mummy, in my language, about all of these things. When I rang her the words fell out of me; I could not help telling her everything. She listened then, when I paused for breath, said incredible words to me.

'You need to talk to my daughter, Deborah.'

'She can talk?' I asked, amazed at this.

'Of course she can!' her mother laughed. 'She has the cochlear – she can do anything!'

When we Skyped, I could not believe it. She was so beautiful and she could speak perfectly. She had a degree in economics - the first deaf person to get a degree at her university. She travelled between London and Milan working in finance, she had a boyfriend, and was so happy. She let me laugh for the first time in however long. I had never seen a cochlear on a person in real life before, with only the little girl in the film Terri showed me as any benchmark at all. This young woman's mother had travelled by train to Milano - fifteen hours every month - for years for her daughter's treatment. She was the third positive person I had met, alongside Terri and Dr Roland. It gave me hope - if she could talk in this way, maybe my boys could do that too. Ale had no chance to talk to her as he was away, but his parents were sneaking a look from behind the door as they were suffering too. I remember Ale's parents that day, they were listening to me talking to this beautiful Italian girl over Skype and it made them so happy, so reassured.

I needed positive people and I was so lucky to find them. At times, the fear when I went to sleep was like a punch in my stomach. I'd wake and think I was dying. I had constant nightmares and I was very insular, thinking, *why me, why do we have to battle all this? I am just a normal person, why my kids?* When they slept, I cried when I looked at them. Even now, I remember that feeling. I was scared and alone as Ale needed to work; we needed the money, we needed the health coverage.

I got a boost speaking to positive people but when I was on my own, it all seemed overwhelming. We had planned to move from the USA at some point, to give the children experience of living in different cultures, and I would also go back to my career, but all of that seemed lost now. We couldn't go to Europe as there was such a waiting list for AVT and cochlear implants, and I felt we were on a schedule at NYU which meant we had to stay there. If the plan for the boys was as tight as Terri said, if I could not afford to lose a day, then we had to stay. And my career? I could never see that I would go back to that at any point. Just when we thought we were about to have everything, all of our opportunities had disappeared. It felt like a punishment.

'Why has this happened?' I asked Dr Roland. 'We are not bad people.'

'We will check everything,' he replied, 'but you need to stop thinking about *why*. It helps no one. Just look at what needs to be done and find the strength to do it.'

I looked at Zack and Dylan at times and felt my heart break. They were so tiny, and they should have been living in a soft cocoon in their first weeks. Instead, they were being subjected to a barrage of tests and assessments. The truth was, they had been tested since the first day of their lives and they were often exhausted too, being woken up from baby slumber for more examinations. We were constantly in appointments and meetings, always at NYU, always speaking to some expert or other. I was a zombie. I remember sitting in the café of NYU one morning thinking, *everyone is here for an illness*. I don't know them, but we all have something in common, especially the mums. It can never be for good reasons. I did have moments of darkness, I had awful thoughts that I couldn't cope, even wondering if I should kill myself. It felt completely unreal. It is a cliché to say that you think some things are a bad dream, that you are in a living nightmare, but that is the reality of some situations. I would look at other babies, other mums, on the streets of New York and think that they were so lucky. My boys were cursed. I was cursed. I had wanted too much, and I had paid the price.

I dressed in black every day, as if I was in mourning. The boys had no nice clothes as there was no time to shop for them, no time to be happy at the prospect of buying lovely things. When we got Keisha, we bought her everything; it seemed like we were in Gap every day. All of that had gone now – in fact, it had never been there, not even for one day. It was so painful and I was not Superwoman. People would call and say, 'Oh, how are you today?' I wanted to punch them; how could they not see how hard this was? I cried when I looked at Dylan and Zack – can you imagine that? Crying at the sight of your own children? But it hurt so much. I had no voice and thought that I had no ability to cope with this.

It is true that you have to reach the bottom before you can climb, but if I had known then just how far I had to fall I'm not sure I would ever have coped at all.

CHAPTER NINE
BELIEVE

It seemed like almost every day I was going from the 58th floor of our apartment to the subway. I could do those streets with my eyes closed. I'm not ashamed to say that I often cried on the subway; no one is really bothered by anything you do in New York so it wasn't even commented on, but I felt so lost, I just wanted someone to understand.

One day, when Alessandro was home, the five of us went to a gospel church in Harlem. When we came out, the boys were asleep so Ale took Keisha to play and climb in the park. As I was sitting there, a cloud of unhappiness cloaking my emaciated body, an old African-American man sat down beside me. He appeared poor and looked like he had had a hard life. I was just staring into space as he started to talk to me.

'You need to remember there is an old proverb - the spring will always come,' he said to me. He didn't know what I was going through, I can only think that my sadness was very obvious. I don't think I was paying much attention when he first sat down, but my brain registered his words.

I moved my head and said, 'Do you think so? Do you really think so?'

'Absolutely,' he told me, smiling. 'Absolutely.'

Oh, I thought, *maybe he's right.*

At that moment, that old man helped me more than he could ever imagine. I wanted our spring to come so badly, I wanted to have hope. I felt like my father had sent me this old man. Otherwise why, in that moment of despair, did he come? He was gone by the time Alessandro came back with Keisha, and I sometimes wonder if I imagined him. I was desperate when I looked at Dylan and Zack, already thinking of the surgery and whether they would survive.

If I am sad, I don't eat. I was so thin that I looked ill. You could see it in me – I looked like a ghost. Dr Roland did try to assure me the surgery would be fine, but I still felt that my tummy was full of worry. The future terrified me - would the twins talk, go to school, have jobs? What has become clear from this time is that anyone going through bad times needs to invest in themselves. You have to take care of your mind and body as you need to be there for your children. They want you in their lives, so look after yourself to ensure that happens. I didn't realise this at the time and I took no care at all. I washed my face, brushed my teeth, but that was all. I wore the same dress that I had washed the night before. I had abandoned my personal care, but I didn't know that I was building my personality.

Even through adoption, IVF, pregnancy, you must take care of yourself, find the time, even if it is only thirty minutes. Have a bath, light candles, smell the flowers. I did so much but I never relaxed. We lived in a skyscraper with six doormen. They helped with everything when they discovered our problems; they always greeted me with a smile when they said good morning, and assisted with the stroller, but I was flat. Even when I smiled, I was flat. Life changed in many ways. Some friends disappeared. Some were incredibly miserable about it as if someone had died – 'We are so sorry, how did it happen, what went wrong, could you have prevented it?' People called as if in condolence. Their voices were a problem for sure, and I worried that they'd never accept my kids if they reacted this way.

You must avoid the people who will pull you down and choose the ones who will pull you up. Emotional vampires will not help. I wish I had just gone for coffee with people and told them what I needed. If I had spoken happily, they would have taken their cue from me. If I had wanted to cry, they would have cried with me. My good friend Claire was the one who stood by me, and she was the one who wept too when I told her that the twins had been born deaf. You need different friends for different things, and she was just what I needed for that.

People can also surprise you. My mamma and my in-laws were wonderful; they supported me and also respected my silence at times, not asking every question. They were kind and yet I know they were also so scared that I might fall into pieces when Ale wasn't there. They had to learn a new way of being. They trusted me 100% to do the right thing for their grandsons, and they helped make Keisha feel special and involved.

Too often, I felt that I was just holding on and no more - what if something happened to me? What if I got ill? Who would do all of this? I couldn't be depressed or unwell, I just couldn't let it happen, and yet I was obviously falling into that, even if I said it could never happen.

I loved all my children from the moment I saw them and had never once thought they were not mine because they came from the egg of another woman. I needed to hold onto that, to remember how much I had wanted them. I needed to fight for them. I never thought I would get out of this – there was no time to reflect as all the time in every day was for them. Now, I'd say don't worry - an hour away will change you and it won't harm them. These days, the women I work with have the same worries and I know what they will say because I've been there, I understand. I never judge. They trust because I am a mum like them too. I know what they need, but I also know the fear that comes from thinking if you take your eyes off what your children need even for a second, something terrible will happen. At the beginning, as I have said, I did think I was having to pay for something, that I was being punished. In that moment, you are so desperate you wonder about things that, at other times, you would laugh at. I see that in people all the time. The mums really need to talk, but most of the dads don't want to talk or even accept that their child is disabled, or has special needs, in the beginning. They all need to see someone who has got through and I would have loved that as well. If I could have accessed someone who was nearby, if I could have seen them and their child flourishing, I could have known it would all pass, instead of feeling that I was in a pit I could never climb out of. Although, it is a strange thing that if Ale had offered to change places, I wouldn't have accepted. I needed to be in control and do it all. One minute I would be thinking, *how can I change all this mess*? Then the next, *I need to do this, I am the only one who can.*

Looking back, I wondered how I got up every day. I knew I had a lot of strength but the woman I had to be in those early months was a warrior. If I could see that woman, I would tell her I was proud of her. If I could see that woman, I would tell her how brave she was. I'd say to her that she needs to take care of herself, even have a walk in the park, because in three years I never had an hour alone. But would she listen? Perhaps not. It was the worst period of my life, but I have pride that I got through.

I could not have done without the support of a partner who was not making other problems, but that too would have a cost in years to come. Alessandro did need to have dinner on the table when he returned and could not spend time doing household chores, but he had such enormous work pressure as he couldn't afford to lose his job. He never attacked me; he always said he didn't know how I did it.

What I knew was that it was only me who had to get the boys ready for their cochlear implants – and the thing they needed most in the six months before the operation was AVT. Auditorial Verbal Therapy is quite common in the USA, Canada, Australia, and the UK, but not elsewhere in the world. If you restrict your children to one option, you must invest in that option. We were a hearing, talking family and I wanted them to be part of our noise, and it was AVT which offered that option – they would have the chance to learn everything through listening.

We all think our children will be born perfectly and we certainly hope for that. This is why we have scans and tests - doctors are looking out for things which may make the child's life more difficult. Although many pregnancies end in miscarriage, or other forms of loss, you do not go into a pregnancy thinking that will be your destiny. There is always hope. I was not trying to make my twins into something they were not, I was just trying to secure them the best future possible. People judge, and I did not want Dylan or Zack to have their opportunities constrained by someone else's prejudices. That is why I chose to dedicate myself to them and why I knew that it had to be me. An hour losing talk with them through not applying the AVT approach would be an hour that could never be found again. I need to talk so I needed them to talk.

We were a family that talked all the time – it is not the Italian way to be silent or quiet – and I knew that they would struggle if I did not try to get this for them. There was every chance that they would feel like strangers in their own family, or even make a world only for the two of them, and I did not want that. I wanted them to have every chance and I wanted them to be Keisha's equals. I knew it would be hard, but I would fight for this with every bone in my body.

I needed them to react to life and if that meant I had to control everything for the next six months and beyond, then that is what I would do. Terri was always asking me how I was, as well as the boys, as she had obviously seen the huge toll this took on other mothers. I saw her two or three times every week and she was unwavering in her kindness. In one way, we were a long way from surgery, but in another, every second counted, and the clock was ticking. Terri told us that we needed to start with hearing aids. They were important to stimulate the nerve and the boys' understanding, irrespective of whether I felt uncomfortable just because of the prejudice I had in my mind. Once the decision had been made, the aids were available in just three days. As the ears of babies grow so quickly, it was vital to get them in place as soon as possible. The moulds stay the same size as the ears grow, and a gap is created between the two. Their ears were very shallow as well as very small so there was little to set the moulds into. This is a terrible thing to admit, but I was ashamed the first day I walked out with them wearing those things. Our society is based on perfection - we seek it, we admire it - and my boys had a clear sign that screamed they were not perfect at all. The doormen in our apartment block could now see that our twins had a mark on them, the lack of a future, and I feared hearing them mutter 'poor child'. I was scared of prejudice, that is true. 'Yes, they are deaf!' I almost shouted at the doormen as I breezed past. I was dying inside but I had to claim this. In all honesty, I have no idea if people were really full of prejudice, or whether I was the one with the problem, whether it all came from me being ashamed of their hearing aids.

I could hear a continuous noise, like feedback, coming from the hearing aids once they were in place; it would have driven me mad if I had concentrated on it. The moulds were there as a protocol to stimulate the nerves rather than hearing, which could never have happened with Zack and Dylan as they were profoundly deaf. We'd go back, get measured again, moulds would be taken with paste, and then sent away. We'd take them back for a refit, and it would start all over again. I was always attuned to waiting to hear the feedback starting, so worried in case they heard the noise and it would drive them crazy. Terri said there was no way that they could hear it, but I dreamt about that noise, I imagined it. It was awful.

We were in a constant loop of fitting and refitting as babies grow so fast. They were also moving more so you heard the noise more. They had to wear them all waking hours to stimulate the nerves, and that worried me too. If they moved in their cribs, they would knock them out, and I'd be up again to sort them. I was always on high alert, no matter the time of night or day. I can still hear that feedback noise when I think back. I just kept wondering, *what if they can hear this*? They worked on a very high frequency so there was no chance that they could, but I was always asking Terri, 'Are you sure it's not hurting them?'

What upset me was that Dylan and Zack cried like newborns when they were hungry or needed changing, but there was absolutely no babbling at all. I remembered what Keisha was like when she first came into our lives and it had been so different. Yes, she was a thoughtful child, always watching things, but she was so curious. These boys were not curious at all – they did not react to or connect with anything. Keisha had always been looking for something that took her interest and her chatter, even before she could talk, had been a delight. The twins were just locked in a silent world where they could not do any of these things. They could not react as there was nothing for them to react to. We loved them so much, but we needed to get to six months as that was when their lives could truly begin. I always knew they needed to become fighters; the world would have so many challenges for them, but they didn't know that yet as the world was something that they had no connection to whatsoever.

Terri did not know how much they could hear, although she suspected it was nothing, or very little if that, so we started AVT at five weeks. They would get fed, put on the floor, get moved backwards and forwards to hear toys, usually vomit with all the movement, then need to be fed again. With the first AVT therapist, we had to fit into her timetable, and the only slot she had was 2pm – just when the babies wanted to sleep. There was no other option – we had to take what she had. It'd sit on the carpet with them and sing to them. They did react a little, but it was not because they could hear the singing, it was because their eyes could see the colours or they could feel the toys. This reassured me somewhat as it meant they had no problems with their other senses, hopefully. I was mentally and physically exhausted but I sat there, doing everything I was told as I was so desperate for a reaction. I would sometimes try to believe that if they blinked, that meant they could hear something, but deep down I knew that was not the case. My boys were deaf; they could hear nothing.

CHAPTER TEN
THEIR STORY BEGINS

'Maybe you should stick with sign language,' people would say to me, but I was never in any doubt. I had a vision from the first moment I was told about it.

'We'll do the surgery.'

Perhaps others suggested signing because that was all they knew, that was the only option they had ever heard of. Well, for me, as soon as I heard of cochlear implants, *that* became the only option I wanted to run with. I had no time to look online to find out more, so I went with the information I was given. From that point, I was always at hospital. I remembered a saying - you always want the flower with all the petals. Some of the petals were missing from our boys, but we still had the flowers, and we needed to help them grow those other petals.

I was so busy that I could do nothing unless it was to do with my children. I had three under seventeen months, so any research had to be up to Ale as I just had no time. I would throw questions at him, bits of information I had picked up, and he would always reply, 'I'll Google it.' I knew that we could not wait three years, four years, that would be too late. I knew that sign language would not be enough – I didn't want it, I wanted to fight *now*. Doctors told me, 'It's your choice, but you have to act immediately if that choice is the cochlear implant.'

For a couple of days after Terri had done the tests, it was intense. There were issues of language too; our English is very good but it isn't perfect, so I would write words down and check them later. It did seem like another language anyway, all of the medical terminology. Within a very short space of time though, I knew I had to sink or swim. There was so much to do, even just to get through an ordinary day.

This is what my mornings looked like from Monday to Friday:

- 7am wake up
- Check all three children
- Quickly shower
- Grab breakfast – if I could manage to eat
- Wake up Keisha, Dylan and Zack
- Get Keisha dressed and give her breakfast
- Get the twins dressed and give them breakfast
- 8am leave apartment with a toddler and two babies - Keisha on a buggy board, the twins in their pram - feeling completely exhausted from the night (the weeks) before

- Walk to Keisha's nursery at the Rockefeller Centre, ten blocks away
- Spend the walk talking to Keisha, making faces at the boys, being engaged with all three constantly, so conscious that I could not neglect any of them, even for a second
- 8.30am get to the deli near to the nursery and buy Keisha a snack for later
- Go through security at the Rockefeller Centre
- Leave and go backwards to 43rd Street, then to 1st Avenue to NYU hospital
- 9am get to NYU where everyone knew us.

It was like the film *Groundhog Day*. At NYU, I was usually Terri's first appointment of the day; she was so kind and knew how exhausting it all was for me, and that early appointments after nursery drop off were the best as the twins had usually napped on the way there. I remember her hands checking their ears in a calm, reassuring way. A peace emanated from every pore of Terri Shaw. I was lucky to find her. There were always the same questions to address - were the aids working, did they need changing? After a month we would change to going back every six days, but for now the loop continued.

We also often had paediatrician appointments on 3rd Avenue in Upper Manhattan, for vaccinations, eye tests, genetic testing, and lots of other checks between Terri and the speech pathologist, which meant more subways, up and down stairs constantly. Sometimes kind people helped, sometimes they did not. The unpredictability was another factor I had to consider - as far as unpredictability can be considered - as I never knew whether there would be delays if no one would help me lift the pram. The twins always seemed to be crying at those appointments and I sometimes felt my head would explode with it all. Trying to comfort two babies at the same time, who cannot hear you, who cannot be consoled by your voice, is hard. I could not use sweet words or sing to them in a way that would make them stop, I could only hold them and rock them, hoping they would feel my love and the desire I had to keep them safe. It was all they knew, but I wanted so much more for them. I wanted more for all of us.

The routine continued:

- 10am head back home, talking all the time when the twins were awake
- Get home and if they were napping, do household admin, constantly checking insurance with a knot in my tummy - had

they paid, had they rejected the most recent claim?
- Pay any new medical bills, look on Google to see if there was anything to worry about that I hadn't thought of, read everything I could to ensure we were on track with treatment
- Feed the boys, clean them up, get them into the stroller again
- 1pm leave for the appointment with the speech pathologist
- Head for the 44th Street subway from Grand Central to another station, get another subway (usually the elevators were not working) to 1st Avenue
- Hope there would be someone, anyone, to help me each time – generally, no one offered and I spent a lot of time trying to get a double stroller up and down stairs, aching all over, weak from all of this and the stress, and the lack of eating properly or taking care of myself
- Pray there would be no delays - I had to be on time so I often left early and wanted the twins to wake up naturally if possible, but I'd usually have to push them to wake up

- Feed them in the waiting room and burp them to avoid vomit as the speech pathologist hated that.

We saw the speech pathologist twice a week for an hour and she told me what to do at other times. I must be honest and say that I never felt the same connection with her as the one I had with Terri, or Dr Roland. She was a good professional but clearly not used to newborns, and I did not find her to be warm. She was completely inflexible in changing appointments and I felt the boys were never able to do as much at that time of day, when they had been jiggled asleep from their nap and more likely to be sick from all the movement. I feel that professionals really need to understand the stress that parents are going through and work with that in mind. I don't think she was emetophobic as such, but she was obviously disgusted if they ever vomited, and I felt very nervous every time we entered her clinic in case that happened. I didn't stop for the whole hour as I had to engage with Dylan and Zack constantly, trying to keep my energy up so that it would transfer to them, often looking at these babies and thinking, *is any of this going to help?* I had to keep Terri's words in my mind all the while or I would have given up – every moment lost was a moment we would never get back again. These babies could not be left for six months, they had to be stimulated so they could catch up when the cochlear implants went in. They could not be left to vegetate, they had to be the best I could make them.

The routine carried on:

- 3pm the speech pathology appointment finished and we left to get another subway, back to Keisha's nursery
- There were two changes of subway and crossing a madly busy street, worrying about the dirt and pollution all around my precious babies - cabs weren't an option as they never had two baby seats
- 5pm pick up Keisha, often early if transport had no delays
- Start the walk home again, with Keisha on the buggy board, ten blocks back to our apartment, worrying that I would collapse and that no one would know what to do as I was on my own with three very small children
- Engage with my daughter for ten blocks, talk about her day, try to escape the gnawing fear that all this could fall down

at any moment, that *I* could fall down at any moment
- Get home and feed the twins who would be exhausted from their day, so they were trying to fall asleep rather than eat, cajole them constantly, keep an eye on one while feeding the other, making sure he wasn't napping
- Push away the fact that, yet again, I had only eaten on the run, that I was draining myself, that I would soon be depleted of everything if I went on like this
- Play with them all, talk to them all, sing to them all before Keisha's bedtime, trying to keep the boys awake so that I could concentrate on her and hope they would sleep when it was their time
- When they were all asleep, I would never rest, always listening out for them, always in a state of high alert. When I did sleep, I would wake up in a cold sweat, wondering if I had missed something
- 1am feed for the boys, hardly able to keep my eyes open, juggling the two of them, trying not to wake Keisha
- They could be awake any time from 6am, sometimes falling asleep again as I

showered, but often not, which meant more juggling, taking them into the bathroom with me, taking seconds to get myself ready, if Ale was not at home.

I could have wept as I wrote that list. It looks unrelenting, but the reality was a hundred times worse. Such a list does not show my tears, does not even begin to touch on how all-consuming it felt. I was half my size, I ate not because I was hungry but because I was weakened, and scared that I would collapse on my own with them. This is the normal life of someone who has a child with special needs. Your diary is full of hospital and therapy appointments and you feel that will never change to children's playdates and lazy afternoons. Everything is a threat, and you need to adapt from moment to moment. It is overwhelming to do all of that; I wasn't Superwoman, but I had to do it.

New York was not the place it had been before the twins. With Keisha, we had friends round for dinner and we loved to go out with her. When the twins were born, everything changed. Things became complicated with their hearing loss. Without it, we could have afforded a place just outside Manhattan which would have given us a happy, busy, family life, but now I saw life going on without me. I had no energy. New York was too noisy and there was too much going on. I saw the city in black and white, and I had so many fears, with negativity in every pore of my body.

New York was still running as it always had, but I couldn't take part in it. Other people's lives went on, but mine had changed beyond all recognition. We wanted some silence and some peace, not the sort of environment New York has at all.

Ale would try to get back at weekends, and we'd go to the park, pretending all of this was normal. However, even in the park, even in those moments where we were supposed to forget, I was talking with the twins - at them - constantly.

We were living in a 58th floor apartment at this time, and the laundry room was on the 3rd floor. American skyscrapers don't have washing machines and dryers in their utility rooms or kitchens, so that was not an option for me; I simply had to use the one that was so far away. I would handwash my own plain black clothes every night and wear them again the next day, but three small children generate a lot of dirty clothing, so that wasn't an option for them. So, even doing that simple task, I had to carry it all to the elevator, take the kids, wait an hour for the wash cycle to be done, lift it all over to the tumble dryer, wait for that to finish, and go through the whole process of getting us all upstairs again. While it was all going on, I did more Auditory Verbal Therapy with Dylan and Zack, and talked with Keisha too. It was a nightmare; even the simplest of tasks took military precision and planning. I don't resent that Ale was away at work – there had to be someone earning money and making sure we had health coverage – but I don't think he really knew what my days were like.

I was just waiting for the implants and I found I was on autopilot when I had to explain it to people. Cochlear implants are designed to mimic the function of a healthy inner ear, called the cochlea. They replace the function of damaged sensory hair cells inside the cochlea to provide a clearer sound than is achievable with hearing aids. Cochlear implants can seem like a miracle because they provide access to sounds that previously could not be heard, and I wanted this miracle for my babies. I wanted all of the promises to come true, and their lives to begin.

We became experts very quickly. There are two primary components of the cochlear - the external sound processor and the implant, which is surgically placed beneath the skin and attached to a row of electrodes that are inserted in the cochlea. It sounds brutal, but it was our only hope that our sons would not always be judged and always have their lives restricted by the special needs which existed since their birth. We had excellent insurance because of Ale's coverage at work, and that was a blessing. In the USA, if you can't pay, you are stuck. If you are limited in your coverage, you are stuck. This changed everything. Without his job, we would be facing the prospect of losing two years of progress for the boys. The two hour surgery alone would cost $125,000 for each ear, and there were so many associated financial implications.

When I decided that this was the route we had to take, I couldn't help but think that they would only be six months old, still so tiny and vulnerable but facing a general anaesthetic. I couldn't dwell on the emotional side, so I had to concentrate on the practical. In a scenario like that, you just have to do things, you don't have the luxury of overthinking. I did, however, feel sad inside when I saw women celebrate the birth of their babies - I didn't have that. No one even sent a card to us.

Still, I couldn't wallow in thinking about those things – there was a path for us to follow, and I had to focus on that. I do remember thinking, *I'll never work again*. It was as if so many instant decisions about my identity at work, and my identity in relationship to my husband, had been taken so quickly, as if a clock was ticking far too fast. I had never felt like a housewife in my life. I loved my job, but now I faced a crisis of identity. Who was I now? Everything in my vision for our future was shattered. I would not be working in Mexico, taking up the opportunity which had been offered when I was pregnant, I would be fighting for my children. I would not be sending the twins to nursery there when they were six months old – instead, they would be undergoing surgery which would have terrified me if I had given it headspace. We certainly couldn't think of going back to Europe. The waiting lists for cochlear implants were so long that we would have lost two years. In America, everything was instant. Specialists, therapy, hearing aids, and more – you could have it in a day, but it cost a fortune. 45 minutes with a speech therapist was $500 dollars. Everything was, of course, doubled because we had twins. It was a staggering amount, and the fear was that, no matter what, Ale *had* to hold on to his job because without the health cover our boys had no hope.

In the middle of the night, in the darkness, the terror would come. I would fall asleep quite easily, exhausted from the day, but I would wake in the early hours, drenched in sweat, a panic attack upon me. I would see that Ale was awake too.

'This is a nightmare,' I would weep. 'Where are we going with the kids? What will become of them, of us? What did we do to deserve this?'

'If I hadn't pushed you for that last IVF . . .' he would always begin, before I interrupted him.

'No, no! You didn't push me, I wanted this. I wanted siblings for Keisha. I love them so much, but I am terrified for what their lives will be. Did we want them too much, Ale?'

Neither of us were rational in those moments. I felt that we had lost the kids we were supposed to have. It wasn't true, of course, we'd just got different kids. During the night, you see only disaster. The monsters appear and you have no strength to fight them until the light appears again.

When Alessandro would say to me at night, as he had done so many times, 'This must be a punishment because we wanted it so badly,' I sometimes wondered too. We had no religious side, but such struggles make you question everything. I could not dwell on such things though – I had a vision for my sons, and I was already on the path to make their stories the ones we had always dreamed of for them. I needed to dig deep – maybe I could be Superwoman after all.

CHAPTER ELEVEN
SILENCE

For those first two months we searched for an answer, always asking those same questions which had been there from the start. Was it me? Was it Ale? Was it the donor egg? Was it a virus? Was it something in one of our family histories? Was it linked to a distant cousin who was deaf? Was it the medication I had taken in the first trimester? They are fraternal, not identical, so why did both of them have it? That made us think it was likely to have been a viral infection. We wanted someone to blame but the experts were pragmatic. They said we just needed to move on, that the reason didn't matter, and they were right. The genetic tests were all negative – we actually discovered that many parents will never know the reason. Every day that I didn't do something to progress the children, was a day lost.

'The genetic tests were negative,' the experts would respond, if we raised these issues. 'Maybe it was an undetected infection during pregnancy, but we need to move on. Every day is a gap, every day is a potential loss.' But these things niggle, they can eat away at you. Fertility treatment is so invasive, and the only upside is that you feel things are being watched meticulously. Could this have been noticed in advance? *Should* it have been? Even if it had, what we have done? I guess all that could have happened was we could have prepared, we could have done research without the pressure of time.

I felt as if I hadn't slept for years, as if there was always something to be done and that I had to be the one doing it. I am not a superhero, I am not a force of nature, but I am a mother and, as a mother, I will always fight for my children. When this battle came into my life, there were times when I wondered if I would be strong enough, but that is all it was: moments of wondering, moments of such exhaustion that the doubt crept in. During those moments, I was someone else – and I do truly believe that complete physical exhaustion allows negativity to find an entry point – but I always came back to the woman, the mother, I needed to be for my children. I could not be weak, I could not rest for a moment, because I was in charge of their future. If I failed in the early stages, it would affect them forever. I never really saw my boys as 'disabled' and, to this day, I see no child with that label, I just see potential. Once you decide that your child *does* have that label, you are limiting their choices and, with that, condemning them to a limited future. What parent would want that? So, if you want the opposite, if you want their lives to be full of hope and potential, for them to become the best people they can possibly be, you take away the label. Others may try to impose it but you have a duty, as a mother, as a parent, to say that you will not allow that. You will not allow anyone to restrict the potential of your child, and you will fight tooth and nail to make sure they are everything they can be, that you will be there when they realise there are no limits, that they can reach any goal.

I know some people will say that every child is different, every 'disability' is different and, of course, that is true. However, I feel very strongly that the way we approach challenges like this creates an environment in which our sons and daughters can flourish, or despair. If everything you say to your babies is about what they can't do, what they don't have access to, then you are placing limitations on them from the outset. And, if their mother is the one doing that, what chance do they have with the rest of the world - a world which does not love them and cherish them in the same way? We must arm our little ones as they make their way in the world, and that is a message I believe every parent must hear and apply. Don't forget – it is also a selfish message, because if you can go to bed every night knowing you have done this, that you have done all you can for your child, then you will have nothing to regret.

I felt as if I was on the clock with Zack and Dylan. I had four years to give them the strength and the abilities to be who they could be before I tried to get them into mainstream school - which was my goal - and, before that, the six months of Auditory Verbal Therapy prior to surgery. There were so many problems. Naturally, my relationship with Ale was affected. I was working on their therapy from morning until evening. I was trying to create a normal world for Keisha. But none of them saw the despair, none of them knew that I was on my knees so many times. It was a struggle, but there is always hope. I recognised that, while there are limits, you must pay attention to your kids, fill them with passion and positivity and then they will shine. If they are put in a corner, they will stay there. We always thought *they can do it* and believed that in our hearts, even when the day itself had been hopeless. We had to look at the bigger picture.

'Maybe we wanted it too much and we have had to pay for it,' said Ale, returning to one of his favourite themes.

'We cannot think like that,' I replied. 'It is what it is. We can only play the cards we have been dealt.'

When I looked back, I remember that the IVF was such a struggle. It is very tough on both partners, but for the woman the physical toll is immense, as well as the emotional and mental aspects. I didn't want to do that last treatment, the fourth cycle which gave us our boys, but Ale pushed for it. I wasn't sure I could maintain the incredible level of commitment you need, the extreme highs and lows, but perhaps the fact I went through that was preparation in some way. Now that I fully believe everything is there for a reason, I have to acknowledge there was a reason for those difficult times during fertility treatment too. Those times gave me the foundation of strength that I needed – I thought I had been strong before, but there had been nothing to match the scale of this.

Back then, I had needed to learn at every stage, and these were lessons I could apply now. When the pregnancy was terrible with hyperemesis, when I lost so much weight and became so weak I could hardly stand, it actually showed me there was a power in me that I had not imagined. After the boys were delivered four weeks early, there were moments during which our questions did not align with the answers of the doctors, and that was a lesson too. We searched for an answer as to why our twins were deaf – but there would never be one. I also had to learn that Keisha could not be a casualty of this, which was something I knew when I was going through IVF. Often, when a baby is born with a challenge, the other siblings suffer but we involved her in everything and decided that she would have a vital role in their development. I had always taken care of me but, at this point, I was still losing a lot of weight, still dressing in black, and my face was still distraught. I cried myself to sleep every night, usually alone as Ale was away for work. We had only wanted a family, and we had fought so hard for a family, so why this? It is so hard to break away from negativity, but it was that which was pulling me down as much as anything else.

Ale was in another world, not just another country – he had to be there because we could not risk losing his job, but it was another thing to deal with at such a hard time. I had a sister in Milano but I could not rely on her, because when you are far away you can't imagine. I had no time for friends apart from the one. She called me every morning and I was still crying with her.

'Claire,' I would wail, 'why us?'

Sometimes you don't need answers, you need silence. It was ironic that I wanted the very thing which Zack and Dylan had too much of. They were locked in the environment which I craved. I tried to talk with positive people, not the negative ones, but I preferred to stay alone. It was an Everest to climb and not just with one baby whose life was in my hands, but two. I was so happy that we'd had Keisha before this happened, that she'd had so much time at the park where we could give her all of our attention. She had a normal life before the twins, and although I tried my hardest to keep it that way, you cannot get away from the fact that once a family has a child with special challenges, life changes. I was so focused on therapy and doctors, but that wonderful little girl was never jealous, not for one moment. She gave me the strength to move forward every day. She'd put her tiny hand in mine, she came to the hospital when she wasn't at nursery, always patting my arm, always giving me love. She was a happy child and she loved her brothers so much. I guess the truth was, sad though it might seem, this was her normality. She was so young that she probably couldn't remember a time before Dylan and Zack, a time when her mother had all the energy in the world. It was a relief that I could do happy, spontaneous things with her - I don't recall any of that with Zack and Dylan. Keisha gave me the energy to move on when all I could think was whether or not my boys had a future. I was exhausted from talking constantly and she would help me. She could sense what I needed to get through. I truly felt that she had been sent to me.

The doctors gave me the medicine and analysis, the speech therapists gave me the techniques, but I had to provide the fighting spirit. I had always promised I would be the mummy who, if her child said they couldn't do something, would encourage them to find a way. I was the one who needed to do that now. Yet, many doors closed, one after another, and you can't help but change your perception of other people based on their reactions. A friend called us and started chatting about the kids, after being out of contact for a while. When I told her the issues, she asked why we hadn't had an amnio. What was she really saying? That we should have killed them if we had known in advance?

AVT is something you need to start with to stimulate the understanding of the child, to help them to learn how to listen. At the weekends, Ale would work with Zack and Dylan a lot on that, and I would try to focus on Keisha. Terri had told me that it would be unbelievably intensive for the entire six months before surgery, a fact confirmed by the speech pathologist. All of the therapy sessions were based on play, conversation, and more conversation. I would chatter constantly, even though I knew they couldn't hear me, as it was so important to stimulate the nerve before the cochlear implants. The fact was, we hear with the brain and not with the ears. We had to work on their understanding before their speech.

'Oh, what is this?' I would say, picking up a ball. 'It is so nice and round, it can roll when we push it, it is a ball. Yes, it is a ball and we can play with it and we can throw it. Do you see? And what is this? It is a toy car, and it has wheels, and we can push that too. And what of this toy? It is a teddy and it is so soft, and we can hug it. The teddy is here, do you like it? Do you like the teddy and the car and the ball?' Holding each item up in front of them, trying to make connections, trying to show them how communication worked so that when they had the opportunity themselves, they would know the patterns and conventions. It was exhausting; hour after hour of chatter, lifting one toy up after another too. I think it was the unnatural element of it which was so draining because, of course, you would talk to and play with your babies in a natural setting. However, being watched by someone who was taking notes, feeling that you were performing, is a completely different matter. And everything was silent, apart from me – I became sick of my own voice, and so conscious that my boys did not react. If they had no eye contact with me, I could not engage them unless I put a toy directly in their line of vision. I knew this all needed to be highly focused in order for them to develop skills of listening and speaking, but I sometimes feared I was doing no good at all. I tried to keep Terri's words in my mind and tell myself over and over, *you cannot lose a minute, you will never get this time to make a difference back again as they will never be at this particular moment of their development.* It was so important to start stimulating the kids to listen even before the implantation, and I couldn't lose sight of that for a second.

I did feel alone while Ale was in Mexico City; even though he was coming home at weekends, we were both exhausted by then. I had been with the children all week and had got into some routine, then we were faced with quite an unnatural situation of trying to fit a whole week of our relationship together into two days. On top of that, he had friends who were telling him theories about medicine, and what could 'fix' our boys. I was in the middle of medicine and tests and science, I knew we had chosen the right way and so did Ale, but he was bombarded with people trying to convince him otherwise. Babbo had been a doctor so I had no health anxiety as such – my worries at this time were about the future, not whether it was intimidating to talk to professionals. That never crossed my mind. Doctors were never a scary breed for me, but this was a different battle. I was used to doctors, and I was strong, as was Ale – a strength we both needed to draw on. Ale's parents have always been more scared about mental issues, medicine and doctors. He is more anxious in general, and this affected him. I was never scared of the surgery because, as I said before, my background helped so much with that. Your upbringing makes sense at moments like this. It was all giving me the strength for a battle I'd never known I'd have to fight.

I would speak to my father, who I missed so terribly, in the night when the panic swept over me.

Please help me, please help me, Babbo. It is terrible for me to know my kids can't hear, that I cannot know whether they will ever escape their world of silence. After what happened to you, I thought that life would be kind to me. There was such a wall to climb when you left, but now there is another in front of me, and it seems bigger than ever. It seems impossible.

I wanted hope from him. I wanted him to be there beside me, making it all better.

While we waited for the cochlear implants, it was important to still see Terri, for hearing aid adjustments, and the speech pathologist. I was counting the days. The implants were to actually be done at seven months, but we thought of it as six months as our boys were four weeks early. I was warned that they couldn't catch a cold or any infection, and that they had to be as strong as possible. This meant that we couldn't stay in New York for winter, and neither could we go to Italy, as both places would be too cold. Instead, we went to Mexico for a week. We felt a little alone, but we needed the heat to keep them well. They got strong in the sun with so much Vitamin D, but I was so scared of the hearing aids going in the sand. They were still not crawling, so we had to hold them all the time or lay them on towels. Even on the beach, I did therapy constantly. Alessandro spent most of the time with Keisha to keep things normal for her, and they did a lot of swimming, but that was something else Zack and Dylan could not do. It was tiring, checking the hearing aids all the time, always doing AVT; they sometimes smiled but they were lost in their world of silence, with little mobility and no interest in anything.

I also had to apply the AVT techniques to everything outside of the speech pathology sessions too. Whether walking from Keisha's drop off at nursery or her pick-up, I would chatter, chatter, chatter. People must have thought I was mad if they passed me regularly, they must have thought, *does that woman never shut up? Her poor children listening to that all the time!*

Listening had to become part of their silent world. It seems completely contradictory, but it had been shown to work, and it was all I had to cling onto. I couldn't take it easy because I only had one option. I had to choose - and I chose them. I told myself that I would get another job in the future, even although I knew it wouldn't be easy. I'd need to reinvent myself, but I would deal with that when the time came. I do feel that Ale and I lost part of ourselves as a couple too; we were never anxious people before, or ones that worried about the future, but this changed everything. It is usually the mamma who deals with situations like this, and the papa stays at work, and I didn't resent that. I could not see that anyone but me would do this, so I never blamed Alessandro for fulfilling a different role. I was obsessed, and that left much less room for him, but it had to be done. I had to achieve this at any cost. All I could speak about was the boys, hearing loss theories and treatments. If we ever went out - which was incredibly rare - I would look at the relaxed faces of people with such envy. All that was in my mind was what I could do next for my children, all of them. I was sleepless, white-faced, always dressed the same way, and never present. Other people would be talking about politics or art or television, but my only topic was deafness. It consumed me. I thought that people with little problems were stupid, and I think that was because when we all face problems in one way or another we close ourselves off. However, no one was obliged to understand my problems, and I had to come to terms with that.

My mother was calling every single day.

'OK,' she'd say. 'You know that in Italy we have a saying for this, don't you, Deborah? Hope is the last to die. That is what you must hold on to. Be as positive as you have always been. Keep hopeful and you will get through this. We all trust what you and Alessandro are doing, so just decide what is next every day, and keep some hope in your heart.'

Dylan and Zack needed to have MRIs when they were four months old at NYU. I knew that building all too well. As I took them to the fifth floor early one morning, I was praying that this would work, that their auditory nerves would be eligible for the cochlear implants – nothing was guaranteed. They were being auditioned as candidates really. If the nerve worked and the brain worked as they needed to, if all the checks for other disabilities were fine, then the implants would go ahead in two months. I was so nervous as we needed the right results.

Dr Roland read the MRI. Looking at the computer screen, he casually scrolled the layers with a mouse. I was just praying that the nerve was there for each of them, for without it another door would slam in our faces. He was so kind – knowing that my anxiety was horrendous, he immediately told us the results.

'All is fine, Deborah and Alessandro,' he said, calmly. 'Everything will work out – my team will be in contact with you to tell you the date and details, but you can breathe now; the implants *will* go ahead.'

In that moment, you see a day when you can be born again. The surgery would begin their lives. It was such a huge relief and it also made me think, *right, I can do this - we can start them on the right path as they will have the capacity to do it*. It would be time for their silence to end, and I would glory in the sound of my boys playing together, hearing the world for the very first time. I had to keep fighting - I couldn't stop now - but I could finally see that there may be some light.

CHAPTER TWELVE
SURGERY

Around this time, the company Ale worked for told him they would no longer pay for our New York apartment – he was in Mexico more than he was in the USA, so they had no obligation to continue with that side of things. This was such a shock to us. The rental was $6,000 every month, and there was no way we could find that sort of money – but there was also no way that Alessandro could leave the company as we still needed them for all of the health coverage.

The decision had to be made and we had no option really. All of us moved to Mexico in January 2012, and the tables were soon turned; I would have to be the one who did all of the travelling. I was happy to go as it seemed a very positive thing, much more in line with how I had always wanted to live my life, seeing other cultures and different people, but I was also very scared. There was no audiology department nearby, in fact there was nowhere suitable in the entire country. I had no contacts there and I did not want to start all over again. NYU was my only point of reference and I would have to travel back there for all of the appointments, taking the boys on the plane alone, navigating everything, until they got the implants. It was overwhelming to think of, so I tried to just break it down into steps. We were not aware of how many times I was going to have to go back after the implants, but I couldn't think that far ahead. We both completely underestimated the impact it would have on me. Each trip meant that I'd be away for two days at a time.

When you go through something as major as your child, or children, being diagnosed with a lifetime condition, it takes time to process, even though you are thrown into it. You can be helped within that process, but we had no psychological support at all. So much pain could have been avoided if that had been in place. If someone had just said, 'You can't change what you can't change,' and we had listened, then we would have been out of the starting blocks like a shot. That is the message I want to pass on, that is the legacy of what we endured.

I was so happy that we had Keisha in our world before the twins were born – she had a normal life at that point; we would go to the park, we would focus on her. Once you have 'disabled' kids, everything changes. All I did was focus on therapy and doctors in New York and I was going to do the same while we were in Mexico, just with added travel. Every day. Every single day there was AVT and a sense that there was another journey ahead. There was a huge sense of urgency as, with deafness, you have no time.

We had hit the ground running and had never been able to just wallow in the glow of having newborns, and that was still the case. With Keisha, we'd had such fun in places like Central Park, laughing and playing. We'd had no time to do that with Zack and Dylan and now we were on the move again. I would be facing a flight of almost five hours each way, added to that would be travel to and from each airport, check-in times, all the stress of getting prepared – I honestly had no idea how I was going to do it. With a child who had no problems, it would be hard. With a baby, it would be harder. With a baby who had problems, so difficult. With twins who could do nothing, hear nothing, it looked impossible – but I was used to the impossible by now. It was just another mountain to climb.

For the first seven months, it was hard to not fall into the negative thoughts – what had we done to them, and why were we still putting them through so much? By bringing them into this world, we had destroyed them – it was a circular way of thinking, but there were times when it was so hard to pull out of, to see the truth. I had a coach by this time, someone to try and help me see my way out of circular thinking, but it was hard at times. Dylan and Zack could only *not* have been in this position if we had never conceived them in the first place, and that was something we would never wish. We couldn't imagine life without them, but it was terrible to live that way. When I was with the twins, I was often on physical autopilot, while my brain raced ahead. People ask about my mental health during those days and I am quite clear about what my state was – I was obsessed, not depressed.

The key was to be resourceful. Running through my brain, constantly, were the words of a doctor who had said, 'TIME. It's all about TIME. Lose a day, a week, a month, and they will be behind.' If I wasn't thinking of his words, I was thinking of the video they had showed me of the cochlear implant, which could only happen after the babies had worn hearing aids for six months. There was a clock ticking all the time.

Surgery was scheduled for the 25th of February 2012, so we all returned to New York four days before. We stayed with a marvellous friend called Amparo – the grandparents too – and it made us feel so loved at such a time. Being in New York brought back vivid memories. I had walked those streets so many times, almost dropping from exhaustion, constantly chatting to Zack and Dylan while trying to keep Keisha amused too. It was in the past now, and the future was in the hands of Dr Roland and what I could do for the boys afterwards.

The snow was high when we got there, piled up on the edges of the sidewalk. New Yorkers bundled up in so many scarves and coats and layers that you could see few faces. Each day we trudged to the hospital as the boys had to undergo three days of checks before their operations. We all stayed together and went as a gang, which was so different to the journeys I had made before with all three children and no one to talk to. I think it was when Zack and Dylan had to get blood tests for their anaesthetics that it hit me. They were so little and yet they were going to go through an operation with a general anaesthetic. I felt so protective of them; even though I was pushing them constantly they were, of course, just little babies, not even toddlers yet. They could not understand what was happening. Although, in some ways, that could be seen as better as they would have no concept of what was coming. However, it did make me feel that they were terribly vulnerable.

'We will put a mark on their ears where the implants need to go, they will sleep, and they will wake up as different children. The surgery will be at 8am,' said Dr Roland, 'so make sure you are here at 6am.' It felt like the morning of their birth all over again. At that appointment, I took a picture of the boys lying on a hospital bed, oblivious to everything. 'Well, guys, are you ready? Tomorrow you start your lives!' I had wanted that for them for all of these months and it was overwhelming to me that the moment had almost arrived. At 7pm on the night of surgery, I did so much therapy. Until the last moment before they went to sleep, I was still chattering away, still trying to engage with them, still obsessed.

The next morning, Alessandro and I arrived at the hospital with the boys, the grandparents looking after Keisha, again, just like on the day they were born only six months before. It was all so similar. Back then, I had been excited to meet my babies, the children I had wanted for so long, not knowing that all our dreams would be shattered so soon. On that day, I went into the operating theatre and saw all of the medical staff, the team for each child who had to be ready for any emergency, but I had felt more in control then than I did now – I wouldn't be in that operating theatre with them, I wouldn't be able to hold them while they went through this procedure.

The waiting room was so cold, and it was still snowing outside. It was dark, with heavy clouds that were weighed down. Holding one boy each, I smiled at Ale, and he smiled back – we had to think of this as a happy moment, but no parent can help but feel anxious when their child is facing an operation. 'It will be fine,' said Alessandro. I knew he was right – I hoped he was right – and that all of my efforts had led us to this. It didn't stop all of my nerves, but I concentrated on the positives.

We were called upstairs to another little room where we were met by the head of nursing. She made sure that the boys had no runny noses or any signs of a cold at all, and then it was time.

Dylan would be first.

She took him in her arms and waved his little hand at us. 'Say 'bye' to Mommy and Daddy!' she told him but, of course, he could not hear.

In that moment, it hit me again. *Wow – I am going to give my child to surgery and I am completely powerless now.*

We sat with Zack, waiting for Dylan's operation to be over. Dr Roland and his team would be doing both, so all we could do was sit there. I had not fed either of them since the night before as their stomachs had to be empty, and Zack was not happy about this. Having not eaten since 2am, he was now starving. We tried to talk to him and distract him and play with him, but he wouldn't stop crying.

After two hours they finished Dylan and he was brought back to us, almost awake. Terri the audiologist had called the week before to say she loved them so much and would be asking for the day off to assist Dr Roland. She was such a kind person. She was true to her word, even though she would not be paid for this, and it was she who entered the room with Dylan, with Dr Roland following closely behind. They were both smiling and seemed very happy.

'Here you are,' said Dr Roland, grinning. 'This one is ready for school!' I was full of relief, and his words made me think that, finally, this could all be possible. That sentence stayed with us. We could change our lives. There was a bandage on Dylan's head, so we couldn't see the cochlear implant, but Dr Roland assured us that all of the electrodes were working. The internal 'work' had all been done and they would be switched on in three weeks, once everything had healed.

'Everything went perfectly,' Terri agreed. 'When the electrodes were put in, Dylan heard the sound from the computer and reacted.' I was smiling and nodding, but these words! These wonderful words! Dylan had reacted, which meant that he had heard something to react *to*.

Zack was still screaming when they took him in, but Terri gave me a reassuring look as if to say, *don't worry – he's next for this miracle!* Her presence was really important to Alessandro and me. Terri had always been so sweet, the type of professional you are blessed to have in your lives. When we had arrived and given her the hearing aids that our boys would no longer need, we told her that we wanted them to go to another family, someone who could not afford them. We later discovered the family who had been given them. The mother was so grateful and actually wrote an amazing social media post about us; it was an extraordinary moment. Terri hugged us, and in that moment – before surgery began – I knew that I would never forget her for the rest of my life.

We were so relieved when Dylan started to come round, and he was so much better by the time the door opened. And there was Terri again, with Dr Roland, and again with one of my babies.

'All has gone ideally,' Dr Roland announced. 'Here we have the other brother ready for school!' I could have wept, or danced, I'm not sure which was more likely!

Ale and I both had masks, scrubs, and plastic shoes on, but our parents had to be outside in the waiting room with Keisha. She was kicking and screaming wanting to see her brothers, but that was impossible as there was an infection risk; in fact, I couldn't even leave the room we were in to comfort her because I had to be cautious of my infection risk too. I could hear her wail and thought again, *Keisha is the one who is feeling all of this – she is the one we need to ensure doesn't lose out.* I wanted to get to her so badly.

Dr Roland had a very difficult seven hour ear cancer surgery to do next, and I realised that was probably one of the reasons he always seemed so positive about our boys – to him, this was going to be a happy ending; with others, that was not always the case. If you have a problem with your child, you are actually very lucky to have a diagnosis like ours. Many are not so blessed. I also know that, to many reading this book, we must seem incredibly privileged. The educated couple from Italy, who had just managed to travel the world, who had a wonderful life and apartment in New York when they achieved their successful adoption of a beautiful little girl. The couple who could afford someone to help out in Mexico City, who had supportive families, who got the best doctors because they had the best health plans. The truth is, we *were* privileged with all of that. When your child has something wrong, there is a levelling amongst parents in that position, but I would never deny that things could have been so much worse. The thought of a mamma going through what I went through in a home that was damp or cold, with no food on the table, in a place that was unsafe, knowing that she could not afford the experts her baby needed…that breaks my heart. In a good hospital, if you have the money, you can just keep going, and we had that luxury. My caesarean had cost

$30,000 but that was nothing compared to how much treatment for the boys was going to be – we estimated it would end up being in the region of a million dollars.

At this moment, however, nothing was about money – it was all about relief and love. We gave a thumbs up to our family behind the glass and could see that they were all in tears. Finally, they were allowed in – not Keisha as she was the biggest infection risk given that she had been in a nursery environment, but the grandparents; only to look, not to touch, and with plastic covers on them.

They were very emotional, seeing their beloved grandsons with bandages on their heads. Finally, Alessandro and I were allowed out to see Keisha, once the boys were asleep and it was obvious they were recovering well. I was so desperate to hold her again, while a nurse looked over Dylan and Zack. My daughter had been so good really, in the middle of even more upheaval. Still, she was only little herself and her tears soon disappeared – I remember that her priority was to get a Kinder egg! All of my worries about her traumatisation were nothing in the grand scheme of a small plastic toy inside some chocolate!

For those first two days, we had to stay with Zack and Dylan while they were fed through an IV drip. In the room was a bed for me, a couch for Ale, and high cribs for the boys. They had to go on strong preventative antibiotics for two days, a nasty, thick pink liquid that they hated. Even more checks were done during that time, but at least we were told that Keisha would be allowed in to visit on the day after the operation. However, that night, just as we started to feel things were going so well, and that we would all be together the next day, Zack developed a fever.

Another doctor, not Dr Roland, said it was perfectly normal and would only last a day, but he started to vomit. All I could think was how I would have felt had I gone back to the hotel and received a call to say this was happening. Thankfully, we were there, but that also meant I saw every time it happened – each time he woke up, he was sick; each time they tried to feed him, he was sick. The nurse also said not to worry, but we were scared to pick him up. In fact, we were scared to pick either of them up in case we made Dylan ill too by moving him.

That was a night of worry. The fever didn't break until the morning – just as the medical staff had anticipated – but we slept very little, always checking on them, always looking for signs that the fever was getting worse or that both of them had it. Despite all of this concern, I never, at any point, thought they might die. Maybe it was because I had become so medicalised; certainly nurses, doctors and hospitals were my normal now. Also, I knew there were no alternatives, they needed to be in the world of sound and it was clear to us that we needed to do it now, so we'd take any risk. A little vomiting didn't seem so bad when I looked at the bigger picture, but we all panic in the moment.

Once the fever had broken and the vomiting had stopped, a doctor came in.

'And how are these boys today?' he asked. 'At school yet? No? Ah well, soon, soon. Now, I have asked for the bandages to be removed from their heads in a little while. Let's see how things are progressing.' It seemed so quick! We were straight back to worrying about problems. Surely it was crazy to remove the bandages when only twenty-four hours ago they were going into surgery? 'Not at all,' said the doctor. 'They need cleaning every day, and we need to air the wounds.'

We could hardly believe it would be so swift but, as soon as the bandages were taken off, both Dylan and Zack seemed to feel better immediately. For the rest of that day they just seemed to improve in leaps and bounds. They were so little and had absolutely no comprehension of what had gone on that I guess, unlike adults, they just reacted in the way they felt, rather than get worn down by worries and fears. After staying two nights, we were allowed to leave and, by that time, they were already improving.

'Am I imagining this?' I asked Ale. 'Do they seem so much better already?' It was hard to tell because, of course, they still could not hear, but they did seem brighter, playing with the new toys Keisha have given them. We were sent home with antibiotics and told there would be a lot of tummy upsets – there certainly were, and Zack in particular screamed with cramps. We couldn't use the hearing aids as they wouldn't work any longer – and, anyway, I had given them to Terri for someone else – so we now had an agonisingly long three-week wait until the implants were to be activated.

For one week, we stayed in New York with Ale's parents and my mamma. We filled the time with walks in the snow and toy shop visits for Keisha, but I wanted to stay indoors a lot as it was bitterly cold, and I feared the boys would get ill. I still did AVT as they needed the contact vision, and it still consumed me. After a check-up six days later, Dr Roland confirmed all was well and we went back to Mexico City for two weeks.

While there, on March 9th 2012, the day Keisha turned two, we decided to have a little party for her, this wonderful girl who had come into our lives like a gift. We needed a celebration and we needed normality. It was a glorious afternoon, with lots of laughter and happiness. As I threw myself down on a chair after dancing with the birthday girl, I looked over at Zack and Dylan. In their seats, in the middle of all the joy and noise, they could hear nothing. It didn't touch them in the slightest.

'They are zombies,' I whispered to Ale. 'Look. They are so sad. They don't know anything that is going on, they are not part of this. This will be their world. If we don't fight for them, this is how it will always be.'

It strengthened my resolve more than ever. I could not have my babies locked out of life for the rest of their time on Earth, I could not have them being onlookers. I would fight like a lioness for these children, for all three of them, and I would make sure they could climb any mountain, fight any fight.

But, for three weeks, it killed me. They had nothing but a silent world. I looked at them and thought, *that is what your whole existence would have been.* It was awful - they had nothing and I wondered whether they would ever have a life. Is this what it would be like? If the implants didn't work, this is what they would be condemned to. I would still fight, I would still do all I could to give them the tools for an incredible life, but I didn't want them to live in a world of silence. We wanted our boys to hear everything and belong to the world around them.

We went to Keisha's nursery a few days later and all the kids were screaming with happiness, but not Zack and Dylan. They had smiles but there was nothing touching their world. At least with the aids, there was something. You can't explain to a baby why even the little bit has gone, you can't tell them to just wait a tiny bit longer because you are doing all you can. In those moments, I could see what their destiny would have been, and my heart told me that I could fight forever to give them what they deserved, what they needed, and what they would now have.

CHAPTER THIRTEEN
THE SWITCH

We were at the airport going to New York on the 17th of March, for the switch on the next day, when we realised that Zack clearly had a fever. Terrifyingly, his head was swollen so much we could actually feel liquid on it. I called Dr Roland from the airport to tell him we were on our way, but what should we do, should we still come? He was not the one who would do the momentous switch on - that would be the audiologist - but he was the one I automatically went to in a crisis.

'I can see you before the audiologist does,' he told me. 'I can check whether it's still possible to go ahead Don't worry, it'll all be fine.' I am sure that, often, medical professionals don't know the power of their words. They can make a throwaway remark, but you replay it, unpack it; did they mean that, was there a hidden message in there? Equally, when they reassure you, it is like the word of God.

Minutes after we landed at JFK, we got a taxi to Dr Roland's fifth floor office. As soon as he checked, he said, 'I can tell you straight away, this is nothing to worry about – it is just liquid from the operation.' The relief was huge – this meant it could all go ahead as planned. We went to another building, up to the 7th floor, for the next step, the biggest step of all, really. By chance, it was also the same building where we'd had IVF. Terri arrived again, saying, 'I want to see the activation of my boys!'

We had been told by two audiologists that the reaction might not be what we expected. The twins were going to be shocked and they might cry, be curious, or even fall asleep. Honestly, we wanted perfection. Zack was actually already asleep when I took him in, while Ale waited outside with Dylan. I could not wake him at all, but the audiologist said there was no need - a far cry from when I used to attend speech pathology appointments and have to jiggle the boys so much that they were sick.

I held my breath as they put the actual external cochlear onto Zack, then connected it to another cable so the computer could create a threshold of sounds which he would be able to hear. He slept through it all, which was a bit disappointing!

'It doesn't mean anything,' Terri told us.

Dylan was crying by this point too, and he also had no reaction either.

'Is this how it should be?' I asked. 'Shouldn't they be doing something? Shouldn't there be some sort of reaction?'

'No. Remember I said that this can often be the way?' The audiologist smiled. 'Really, every child is different, but they can hear everything. Don't worry at all – come back tomorrow and we'll move onto the next stage.' It was a bit of an anti-climax but that didn't really matter, we would just have to wait and see.

For the first three months after the switch on, I would have to take Zack and Dylan for regular appointments which were called 'mapping'. They were not used to being hearing children, so the audiologists had to open a new sound every day through mapping, which gave them a baseline to work with and also slowly introduced the boys to sound. Some of the sounds were high frequencies, some low, but it was all at a low volume to start with. If the twins got upset by any noise, then the mapping would change; it was all about finding the right level for them.

With this information, we left, and they slept. When they woke up, I was sure they could hear us. They were so relaxed, and I could absolutely see that they were receiving sound. Their eyes were different, they looked alert, and they were moving their heads around, hearing traffic in Manhattan. It wasn't an illusion. Before, an ambulance could go past right by them and there would have been no reaction whatsoever. We had always hated the noise of that polluted city but we loved it that day, we actually wanted fire alarms so we could see their reaction. We took them to a huge toy shop, which was full of noises, and I remember Zack and Dylan moving their heads around in the stroller. We never bought a lot of toys but we did that day, we wanted to buy them everything.

We had more mapping the next day, then the next, and the next, and from that moment I realised I would always be on a plane. The audiology team gave me an eight-month plan which said I needed to be in Manhattan every two weeks; the fact that we lived in Mexico City was irrelevant. It was a huge endeavour but I tried to look at it one trip at a time to avoid being completely overwhelmed. The boys were older now and, although things were changing, I hoped that on trips if they were upset or needed settling, I could soothe them more easily with my voice, or stories, or songs. They were also heavier to lift and manoeuvre about. Amparo, our friend in Connecticut, which is forty-five minutes away from New York, offered to put me and boys up again when we had appointments, which was a lifesaver as we would have struggled to afford it otherwise. While the insurance paid for the treatment, there were so many other expenses too.

Thankfully, the boys were American citizens, so we were processed at customs quickly every time. We were soon known by almost everyone. They all started to notice the little, stressed Italian woman with the twins who passed through more regularly than anyone else. The airline staff were so kind, and if there was a space in business class, often let us sit there for the three-hour flight. I was also very lucky that there was usually an empty seat next to me on the journey, which meant that we could spread out. People were thoughtful, and I was so grateful. They all knew my story, even the staff at JFK, and they would wish us luck and check how we were getting on frequently.

The flight was exhausting in itself but once we got to mapping, that took a whole day of checking as well. However, the wonderful thing was that Dylan and Zack had more and more responses at every appointment. AVT was a passion for me, and within a year they understood so much.

One day, we were in the kitchen, doing therapy before lunch. 'It is so dark today,' I chattered to them. 'What can we do? Ah, we need a light. Now, where is the light?'

All of a sudden, Zack said, 'Mum mum mum mum!'

It was one of the most glorious sounds I had ever heard! My baby knew who I was, he had finally said it and I finally felt as if it had all been worthwhile. Dylan took a few weeks longer to call my name but, in the meantime, they were both making it very clear that they didn't want me to go away as they fell asleep. They were absolutely aware that at night the cochlear came off and it went silent, and I can only guess that this took them back to a time in which that was the norm. It was no wonder that they never wanted to return to it.

The cochlear is only the tool to let them hear and listen, but if you don't do the therapy it is not enough. The doctors were clear that we still needed therapy and that AVT had the best results. It had not stopped; I was still constantly chattering to them. We became an AVT family. Wherever we went - galleries, museums, the Frida Kahlo house in Mexico - I would ask them questions. What is an artist, what is this drawing, what is this vase, what is this painting? The difference now was that we were actually starting to enjoy life. It was a novelty for me. I was still often tired but, in between flights, I was definitely more relaxed. I even sometimes had a little time to myself and would go for lunch with Ale, which was a real luxury. Our relationship was improving too, but the honest truth is that in eighteen months I barely kissed him, or gave him my hand. I was starting to get a little bit of colour back in my cheeks and had even stopped dressing like a Sicilian widow, but there was a long way to go.

AVT was an extraordinary experience in our lives, but as the boys got older I realised that I was going to have to approach it in a different way and get more support in doing that. Our journey had shown us that taking this route for a deaf child is about more than the cochlear - that's technology, but AVT is about how you can actually change your child.

My boys surprised me every day. I saw them react, I saw them grow in confidence. I was still very stressed with the trips to Manhattan, but this was tempered by the happiness I felt every time the audiologists switched on a new sound. When I started each trip though, I would think, *here we go again*, and know that I had hours and hours on my own to get everywhere. I'd leave from our house early in the morning with a big double stroller, two growing children, a huge bag of food, changes of clothes, toys to entertain them on the flight, overnight bags, completely weighed down by it, as I had been since the switch on. Their speech was definitely improving but they weren't walking yet. I thought that was a combination of them spending so much time on flights, and my worry that they would fall being transferred to them. The part of the mapping that I remember so well was the one where the boys were put in a room with two boxes in front of them - one on the left and one on the right. Inside the boxes was a monkey and each time the audiologist was clicking a new sound, one of the monkeys was turning around and so the kids would turn their faces. This test is useful to check not only what they can hear, but also to check the localisation of the sound. Every time the audiologist outside clicked the mapping to make the sound come from the right, the right monkey moved down. After a while, the twins knew what was happening. As soon as they listened, they recognised where the noise was coming from. All other kids were outside playing, mine were in a little room with me praying they would turn their heads when the monkey played. That was the extent of the hopes and dreams of those days.

Each time, as soon as I returned to Mexico City, we would be straight into AVT. It was not a place that I belonged to. I love diversity and a rich fabric in places where I live, but we had to live in a compound for safety reasons. It was like a fake Manhattan, built for rich people who liked to shop at malls and have a very narrow world. It was so impersonal and I only had one friend. There are twenty-three million people there and the city is gridlocked. You can sit in your car for three hours and get nowhere.

We did have someone helping us at home - a lovely young woman called Iris. She was passionate about all three kids, always interacting with them when she was there, taking them to the park, trying to get the boys to walk, rather than being distracted by her phone. It was so good when they were with Iris as she always ensured they played with other children. She would tell me that the other mothers made comments about how delayed Dylan and Zack were with walking and talking, and she would reply, 'I don't care – they will end up faster than anyone at everything.' It was true that they were chatting, playing and understanding more than ever, but still I was concerned about their slowness with crawling and walking. I bought tunnels and foam mats to try and encourage them as well as protect them if they fell. I would sit on the other side of the tunnel and try to get them to come to me, but they were scared, especially Zack. Finally, he and Dylan did crawl, but it was only because they wanted to get to me, not because they had any interest in moving. I went back to the paediatrician with my worries and, again, was told that I was giving them anxiety with my concerns.

Then, one day, out of nowhere, they did it. They walked! One after the other, on the same day. I started to see things get better every single day after that, each one an improvement, and I could finally visualise the life I wanted for them in a way that had always previously been my wish. To hear them running and laughing was wonderful - we did have a lot of therapy, but I tried to give them time to be children too. Alessandro was more relaxed than me, always telling me that they were doing great, especially in comparison to what we had before, but I was the one doing the travelling, spending so many days waiting on the mapping to work, constantly doing AVT, and I guess he didn't have that moment by moment awareness of it. I never resented that though; I would have wanted to be the one who did it no matter what. I was the mamma fighting for her children and I wanted to take that role, even though there had been times when it drained every last ounce of strength from me. Ale says he remembers a photo of me and the boys at the beach after the implant, and I was emaciated. I know that happened, but I also know that it was worth it. We knew that we all had to fight together, it was a race against time. It was just a fact, but there was undoubtedly pressure.

CHAPTER FOURTEEN
A WORLD OF CHANGE

When we moved to Mexico City, we met some wonderful people, especially in the Jewish community where we found a lot of love and support. One family in particular opened their culture to us and played a fantastic role in our journey with nurturing and care, helping us to feel less alone. However, I still spent the vast majority of my time concentrating on what I could do for my children.WhatZack and Dylan needed was an angel, and we found one in an amazing woman called Lilian. She was certified and one of the best AVT people I have ever met, a speech pathologist who, thankfully, spent half of her time in Mexico City, the other half in one of the world's most important hearing loss clinics, based in LA. It was a globally renowned establishment that offered wonderful services to young children with hearing loss and supported their parents. We didn't get access to Lilian immediately, but when I found out she was the best I wrote to her husband Pedro, who was an audiologist in Mexico City, as there was no way to contact her directly. He sent me her email address but said that she travelled a lot and I shouldn't get my hopes up. I was desperate, but I had hope; I'd always had hope.

She wrote back to me the day after that email and said she didn't do this type of work any longer, but would make an exception as she was intrigued by the fact we had twins! She came to our house and it was obvious that our story had drawn her in. Her husband loved Italy (he sadly died last year), and she was so beautiful, so elegant.

'I am travelling around the world so much,' she told me, 'but I'll do this.' Lilian had another reason for wanting to work with Zack and Dylan, a reason she soon revealed to me – she had been diagnosed with breast cancer the week before. 'I think your kids will give me the energy to fight this.'

Zack and Dylan always worked in Spanish with Lilian even though she spoke perfect English. She said that Spanish was the language of her heart, and I could understand that because I felt the same about Italian. Lilian emphasised to us that the language didn't matter, it was the understanding that counted. Usually, with hearing loss, you obsess about words; with AVT, words are peripheral.

'Never say that you are tired,' Lilian advised. 'You say: Oh, when I am tired, what do I do? Ah, yes, I lie down, and I sleep. Now, why do we sleep? That is the way to structure your chat with them. Don't sit in front of them, but to the side, and then they will learn how to listen.' I had known much of this but

Lilian took it to another level. To be entirely honest, I had never been entirely comfortable with the speech pathologist. Lilian, on the other hand, was warm and kind and understanding. She was just what I needed at that point in my life. Through her, AVT became my passion rather than my obsession. She was an amazing woman and she inspired me. I didn't think I had ever met anyone quite like her. Over our time together, she went through a huge personal battle but still found the strength to give Dylan and Zack the wings to fly.

With her, they started babbling. At six months, they were silent. At the end of seven months, they babbled. When they were one, they started saying words. We all definitely benefitted from Lilian, and she benefited from Zack and Dylan. She often admitted that she used them as therapy; she saw the fruition of her life's work in them. The AVT with Lilian was once every two weeks, and I saw such changes with her over that time. Some days she would reschedule for twenty-four hours because she'd had chemotherapy and the effects had hit her badly that round. She always dug deep and found something. We became very close, but I really don't know how she did it. She would come to us burned from radiotherapy, but always dressed perfectly, and she'd laugh about being a fashion victim even when she was going through hell. Lilian influenced me so much; if she could do it, I could do it.

She had such awareness and she extended my knowledge of the process I had been applying since birth. The boys needed to understand before they could talk and she was completely in favour of this. When we read Spot The Dog, it was not enough to say, 'book, book, book' while pointing at it. I would very enthusiastically say to them, 'I wonder who is under the sofa! Who can it be? Is it someone who has four paws? Can it be someone we know already who is under the sofa?' Or if someone came to the door, I was told not to just answer it. I had to say to them, 'I wonder who is at the door! Who can it be? Is it Daddy? Is it Lilian? How can we find out? Do you think it would be a good idea to go and see? How can we do that? How can we find out who is behind the door?' Whereas before they had just stared at me, if they had bothered at all, now they were so excited and engaged. Finally, my babies were alive. We never skipped even one AVT session with Lilian, because I felt that, if I lost one, I would lose the equivalent of one month. They had a fever? Give them some Nurofen and let's go. Lilian was coming to our house at 10am once every two weeks, because once they had the cochlear they didn't need it every day. Every time Lilian visited, she would tell me what was needed for the next meeting. She was a wonder and performed miracles – by nine months Dylan and Zack were saying proper words! 'Mamma' and 'Papa' and 'Lilian'.

This therapy was to be fundamental for our lives, and it was fundamental for the twins. You cannot just say, 'You are dirty – you need a shower.' You have to engage the child by asking them the question in the hope they will understand the link between the situation and how it can be solved. 'Oh, you are dirty. What we can do about that?' You become an AVT parent 24/7. You talk in the park rather than leaving them to play, you tell them the name for everything, you never say something simple; it's always quite convoluted. We never even bought a toy for no reason, but after the cochlears we learned how to play and enjoyed it so much. 'Why do you think that happens?' I would always say rather than give them the answer, and because of this we saw them recover it all. It was exactly what Terri had told us from the start – 'Don't worry, they will close the gap.' And that was exactly what we could see happening before our eyes.

I never slept. Nor did Zack or Dylan, really. They changed day and night around and I was probably more worried about trying to ensure Keisha slept so that she could have some sort of normal schedule.

Alessandro had to work, I was flying back and forth to New York all the time, and when you don't sleep you become obsessed by it. If someone had said to me, 'Take these pills and sleep for three months', I would have thought I had won the lottery. You get a new perspective on what and when to do things when there are so many competing demands. I remember thinking that I needed to potty train Keisha so she could be independent and not need me to be with her if she had to go to the toilet, rather than any other reason. There is a different type of support in the USA – if you need something you buy it and everything is very fast. In Mexico, you have to find a paediatrician and then find a specialist. It all takes time. I had to start everything again but I couldn't lose time; I didn't have that luxury.

You lose your ability to not think of the problems as they fill your mind constantly. We thought that after the cochlear it would all be ok. Yes, it was the tool to give access to sound, but AVT gave them the wings to fly. The therapy is extraordinary, it encourages them to think, not repeat. It's not 'cup, cup, cup', it's, 'Oh, this is something I need to drink from, it is a cup'. Next day, 'Oh I am thirsty, what do you think I need to have a drink from?' But, the AVT was not everything. It was a huge part, however, my mind was already running ahead to the next mountain we would have to climb.

I did feel that we were always at the mercy of Ale's work, largely because he – as always – needed to keep the medical insurance in place, but there was nothing we could really do. All of my plans to continue my career had fallen by the wayside as there was absolutely no way I could have managed to combine work with looking after three children, making sure that AVT was sorted, and continuing with all of the trips to New York. I did feel at a loss and completely powerless about all of that, but those were just the cards we had been dealt. However, once the AVT started to fall into place, I wondered if we could maybe take more control of other aspects of our lives. We wanted to go back to an English speaking country and we knew from Lilian and other experts that one of the best places for what we needed was the UK, and particularly AVTUK.

I needed a plan and we agreed with Lilian that she would write to AVTUK and we would not have to wait. Zack and Dylan were twenty months old by this time and I needed to ensure they stayed on track. Many specialists had told us that the UK was one of the best places in the world for AVT. We couldn't really afford to pay for the best schools in Mexico

City, so we decided to go to a country where all the schools were good.

'What shall we do? Where should we go? The cochlear was invented in Australia, is that an option? Or back to America, or the UK, or Canada?' It was true that we liked European schools, so we were drawn to that. All of our children were going to speak Italian and English, which would help them wherever we were, but we needed to think of the whole picture. It had to be England.

CHAPTER FIFTEEN
MOVING ON

We asked Ale's company for a transfer and, luckily, they agreed. Could this be it, could everything finally be working out for us?

Lilian was as good as her word and wrote to AVTUK who replied to say they were waiting for us and would do a full assessment to see where we were starting from as soon as we settled. When we left, she was so sad but so proud of them. Dylan and Zack don't remember her, but I learned everything from that woman and will never forget. In Mexico City, she used to arrive at our house with a black suitcase full of toys and the twins would bounce in their chairs with excitement when they saw her. After we decided to go to the UK, she gave me that case.

'In here, you will see it all,' she told me. 'You will see where you started and where you are now. It will show you everything.' I opened it when we got to England and she was right - our lives were in there. It also hit me that she wasn't going to do it anymore, she wasn't there to walk beside me, and I would never see her again. She was another of the wonderful, strong women I had met on this journey, and she wouldn't be the last.

When we began making plans to head to the UK, there was so much to do. For me, it was just another piece in the jigsaw which would give my boys a normal life, but for Alessandro it was another step into the unknown which would take him out of the path he had thought was the right one - the world of work and decisions and 'success.' It was a strange time. He later told me that when everything was at its height with the children, he just assumed that I would cope with it all, that I was so strong and that I would never collapse. He felt that I would have a ten-minute rant – the warm-blooded Southern Italian in me – then I would move on. He never doubted my strength, and I never doubted that he would pull back from this too. He always thought that we were both driven, but that I was the strongest and most resilient. I guess, looking back, I had made clear decisions about what would happen, about what I would give up to ensure that this all happened for the boys, so we never had to argue about it. I never lose my clarity; I see the path. Ale admits that he overthinks and if he had been asked to choose between sign language and implants, he would have waivered, just because he was not so involved as me in many decisions since he was always away. At different times, we were both going through different stages of the healing process. Inevitably, a couple absorbs from each other during the difficult times as well as the good, and Alessandro admits that he would still be on the treadmill if it wasn't for the kids. There is always a price and he was going to pay it - the price of his constant travel, his bad lifestyle, and the way he over-valued achievements.

Whatever comes in your life, you have to cope with it; things happen for a reason and your life changes. There is pressure, but that is life. I was blessed to have wonderful people on my journey, wonderful women like Terri and Iris and Lilian, but Ale had work. That was it. Only work, work, work. He wanted such a strong relationship and emotional link with the kids but, in many ways, was prevented from achieving that because of the demands which were placed on him by being the one earning the money. This is so often the case for men – of course, many women work and many women have wonderful careers, but when life throws you a curveball with your children, it is largely women who pick up the pieces. As the mamma, I would not have had it any other way, but both Ale and I paid the price for that. When it is happening, you go day by day, hour by hour at some points, and you tell yourself that you will think about it, you will work out a plan, you will sort everything when you get a moment . . . but when can that moment ever come when you are in the middle of hospital and treatment and therapy? Many parents deal with this to one degree or another, and all of them walk through fire to get where they are at the end of it. They will be changed but doesn't that happen to all of us in one way or another when we have a child? If you knew at the start what you were facing, the courage might never come. Perhaps you need pushing into the ocean without agreeing to it, or you will never know that you can swim.

Once we got to the UK, another angel was about to enter our lives, and it has often been those angels who have kept us going when the waters were very rough indeed. We had chosen to move to the beautiful city of Bath, but that meant that we had to travel to other places – for the AVT every two weeks, for the mapping every three months. This time, however, the travel was easier as it was all on the same continent! Even though appointments often meant I had to leave at 6am to get to a 9am meeting, it was still better than a flight from Mexico to New York! In Bicester, our new angel was called Susie, a certified practitioner with AVTUK, and she was amazing. She was passionate about her job and ambitious with the kids immediately.

She was so right from the very start but she was not the sort of person who simply dictated what I was to do. No, she worked with me every step of the way.

'What are your goals?' she would ask me at every session. 'What would you like the boys to have achieved by the next time we meet?'

I know now that she was also coaching me, she needed me to visualise and verbalise what I wanted for Dylan and Zack. She was an extraordinary therapist and she knew exactly what could be asked of them. I would say the goal I hoped for and Susie would agree, then add a little more. I would go home to Ale and be bewildered.

'How can they reach this?' I would ask him. 'How can they possibly get to that point in such a short time?'

'Ah, well, let's try,' he would reply, knowing that Susie always wanted even more for them. And she was always right – after two days, Zack and Dylan would have reached the goal which I had thought impossible, always making a breakthrough. I learned that if Susie could believe, I could believe. It took about a year, but it happened! She had so much experience and had seen many children before, whereas I was scared that they wouldn't manage, that they would fail, so I hid behind not believing in them at times. When I finally realised how ambitious Susie was for them, I joined her – I saw the world opening up for my boys.

Parents of children with special needs have to create their own reality, they have to believe in things that others can't necessarily see. The first person who normally notices a child's difficulty is the mother – with us, we had the medical tests and the medical profession to give us the results, but that isn't always the case. The mother is the closest person to the child, more attentive than anybody else and more sensitive to perceiving any difficulties. The mother often notices a possible difficulty but might not talk to anyone for fear of facing a challenging reality. She lives in silence with this fear and in the first months doesn't know with whom to talk about it. This fear clearly gives her anxiety and sadness, while she tries and looks for evidence to confirm her suspicion. When her fear turns into a problematic anxiety, the mother often consults a doctor, 'just to check'. Often the mother tries to talk about it at home, but in many cases her fear is labelled as 'stress' or being overprotective.

This happens partly because the rest of the family is afraid to accept a child's difficulty, and partly for fear of the opinion of others.

The family often influences everything too, and the mamma is labelled 'exhausted' or 'worn out'. I see this, and I see that women are rarely wrong when it comes to knowing the heart of their child. I have heard so many women repeating to me the words told to them when they had a suspicion: 'All children take their own time to develop; don't stress about it.' This phrase becomes the one the mamma hears repeated by all, and that often leads her to accept it. I think, however, that the voice of the mother and her fears should absolutely be heard and investigated thoroughly. If no one listens to the mamma at the beginning, time is being lost – to the detriment of the child and their development. We have a duty to listen to a parent who has a doubt. We have a duty to listen.

Take the example of a mother who suspects that her newborn baby does not hear. Ironically, few people really listen to her. Few people want to hear a mamma who has this suspicion and so the easiest thing to do is to dismiss her or try to diminish her fears. But what if she is right? What happens to a child who is diagnosed with a hearing problem too late? That child will have major issues in language and cognitive development – and it is an example which applies to any other issue. Women are silenced in this, as they have been in so many things throughout history. It is ironic that even when they are fulfilling the role that many cultures believe is their *only* role, they are still ignored or brushed aside.

An accurate check is a mother's right. As parents, you have the right to ask for a second opinion if no one listens to you. You have to act and continue to search for the truth because what's at stake is your child's future. Nothing matters more than that, nothing in the world.

When we moved to the UK, Alessandro definitely felt the pressure of it all. He could see just how much the boys needed almost every moment of every day, and I think that was a shock to him as he had been protected from some of it for a while. I could see it all coming to a head with him. The strain, the fact that he wasn't enjoying his job, the move; they had all piled on him at the same time and he wasn't the same man anymore. He undertook counselling sessions and went to a psychotherapist, but he did refuse medication and, in retrospect, that was a mistake. I think what he needed to do was to process everything that was going on, and how much he was seeing about the way our lives truly were now. He also needed to acknowledge that he'd been through depression in the past and that the signs were there again. We still weren't making much time for each other. When you have all of these issues to deal with regarding your children, the sad truth is that you can go weeks, months even, without touching each other. It seems like a luxury when there is so much else to do.

At this time, Alessandro was questioning whether he had got to where he wanted to be in life, whether he had the right balance. To some extent, he needed to reinvent himself because he was heading for complete burnout. Before the kids – certainly, before Zack and Dylan – all that had mattered was his career trajectory. I had actually been like that too, but now he had to think about what mattered. His blood pressure was high, his cholesterol was high, and he was spending far too much time doing rather than being. What you commit to rationally is not always what you want emotionally. Alessandro had always felt this pull to be with us, but he had to work. It was a huge conflict which he could only cope with if he broke it down into smaller chunks, telling himself that it was only a few days at a time, but the emotional cost was huge. Eventually, in the UK, this hit him. After fourteen months, he fell into depression. He couldn't think clearly, he had complete burnout, and was so severely affected that he had no option but to leave the company. Alessandro was so depressed, with no energy anymore – he would have to fight with all his strength to be alive again. He had been brought up in a family where his father (who had been a military pilot) was just devoted to work, while his mother just had to take care of the kids. Ale did not want to have this same role. He wanted to be involved with the emotional side of being a parent but, because of our circumstances, he was actually repeating the same patterns from his own childhood. I think he did realise the value of the paternal role in the emotional daily life of the family, for our children and for me, but the practicalities often seemed insurmountable.

I was starting to see things more clearly – I'd always known that my life would be put on hold for my children, and I'd suspected (as I now knew) that I would never go back to my career as it had been. Now that I was watching Alessandro being forced to reassess everything, more things were falling into place. Parents of children with special needs go through difficult moments, possibly more difficult than those of other parents. From the time they receive the diagnosis, life changes forever, and they enter a new, uncharted territory. Agendas quickly fill up with additional commitments that create congestion in the daily family schedule. There never seems to be enough time and you can feel tired, drained of energy, even hopeless.

Nonetheless, there are also very special moments that give you an extraordinary energy, moments when you feel life has come to knock at your door again. These are not miracles, as many people might think, but rather the results of incredible efforts put into the support and development of your children. These are moments to be treasured and celebrated. For example, when a deaf child speaks their first word, or a child with motor skill difficulties takes their first step, they are moments to celebrate with great intensity, to congratulate both child and parents for the efforts put in and to sustain the motivation to strive for continued learning and development. Those children and their parents are warriors and will lead their life with great courage, but it comes at a price. I was beginning to see it was only when you saw that cost as one worth paying, that you could truly move to the place you needed to be in life.

When my sons were diagnosed with hearing loss, I fell the world was collapsing on me, and this was happening to Ale now – much later, but it was still happening. Taking the time to process my emotions helped me find the strength I needed to help my sons on their journey, and that is what adults need to do as well. If we are going to be there to fight for our children, we need to put ourselves as the priority on our to-do list. I had not always done that, and those were the times when I felt completely lost. Although the term 'special needs' refers to a broad category of developmental and learning needs and issues, there is something in common: parents of children with such needs experience great extra stress. I was also watching other women, women who did not have these issues with their children and seeing a great deal of common ground. Women who were going through a divorce or changing career, who were facing the double burden of looking after their children and their elderly parents, women who just did not know how to make sense of themselves anymore. I was in my bubble, but I could still see out, I could still see other women who were struggling just as much, even if it was with other things. I realised just how many of us see looking after ourselves as an indulgence, when actually it should be our priority. If we go down, the whole ship goes down with us. It is not an indulgence to make sure we survive.

As I watched Ale struggle, I knew I could learn lessons from this which would be important at some point – I didn't realise at that stage that I would be committing my life to helping others in this position, but I did know that there were strategies which could help. They wouldn't solve everything, they wouldn't be a miracle cure, but they would help.

Many parents put themselves last until their health becomes impossible to ignore. It takes some time, but in the end parents realise that putting themselves last isn't going to work. It took me a while and that is how I know - from bitter experience.

You must find 'me' time every day, even if only for half an hour. I had been living on nothing, emotionally and physically, for so long before I realised this. Whether it's reading a magazine, a book, having a cup of your favourite coffee or tea, or talking on the phone to a friend, it's vitally important that parents have a moment in order to recharge, reset and prepare for the next challenge. Read inspiring and optimistic books, lose yourself in funny stories. You need to breathe. You don't need to add problems to problems. Ale wasn't doing this, just as I hadn't either.

Since moving to the UK, I had rediscovered my love of exercise, particularly running. It is so important to reclaim your own body and to feel something that isn't anything other than pure joy, to feel a freedom that comes from your physicality and is yours alone. Ale would eventually find that cycling provided him with this feeling, but again, it took too long. If we'd had someone to tell us to always keep trainers in the car, to go for a walk after dropping our kids at nursery, to swim whenever we could, that would have given us time to dream about our own futures as well as theirs. It was only really when Ale started cycling that he found himself – when he started to build his body as well as his mind again.

Find friends. When you have a child with special needs you need to move on with building friends, and you need to surround yourself with positive and inspiring people, supportive individuals who share your interests or problems. When I started choosing my group of friends I discovered that I became more authentic sharing my real life. Ale was wrapped up in work, with people he didn't know since the move, and that is unhealthy for anyone.

We all need to have a break. You need to take a break from your kids and breathe. Parents often talk about coming to a place of acceptance with their child's diagnosis, and I had moved towards the Buddhist idea of not viewing suffering or difficulties as abnormal. When I think of the fact that Zack and Dylan are going to always wear their implants, it takes my breath away, so I try to live in the present, not focus on the long haul. Having a special needs child brings with it a long journey. Parents need to periodically take a self-assessment and ask themselves what they need, what they aren't getting, what they appreciate, and who they need to talk to in order to get more answers. When I feel down, I call my closest friends and I chat and laugh about funny things, not about awful things. We focus on some projects, on vacations, on books, and finally I feel better. I always call positive people. I need to breathe positivity. If you surround yourself in misery, of course it will seep into you and you will be miserable.

I have that wisdom now, but it took a while to get there. If I could have passed it all over to Alessandro, I would have done so, and I would have changed his path at that moment. But, as I always say, we are given struggles so that we can find a way through them, so that we can become the person we are meant to be. This was his moment – this was the fire he had to walk through.

CHAPTER SIXTEEN
GRASPING THE FUTURE

I knew that, in the UK, AVT was still going to be vital to Dylan and Zack's futures. The twins had already made such progress, but it was time for the next step. We decided that, after six months or so in England, it was finally time for me to get a little time to myself, and the only way to do that was for the boys to go to nursery. It started with three hours twice a week, and then we built it up. It was so strange to have any time to myself, but it made me think of how unsure I was about my own future. I had a plan for my children but not for myself.

Things were changing so quickly. We were so proud on the day they graduated, seeing them in their little graduation outfits, and felt that this was one of the defining moments of all that we'd been through. In that moment, they didn't know they had finished AVT. There was always a beginning, a middle, and an end to the process, even if there is no set timetable for those stages to happen. Once you reach a level, you *are* the AVT as a parent. You keep going as a family, but you don't need to go to a place or location. Although we would go for an assessment every two years, there would be no specific structure any longer from this point in our lives. I must admit I felt as if part of my support network was being taken away, but I also told myself, *they can be children now*. I felt a little lost when they started reception school when they were four, but it was all part of the journey towards school. You need ambitious parents, therapists, everyone.

When we started here in the UK with Susie, she saw how much potential they had and agreed that mainstream school would not only be one option, but the best option of them all. What was needed for any of their learning was an education plan. The headmistress of King Edward School - which was in the nursery the boys went to - helped me to draw up what I needed for Zack and Dylan and, in her, I found yet another amazing woman.

When I told people what I was going to try to do – get highly specialised state health and education plans in place for both of my boys, which would provide them with everything they needed for mainstream school – they would look at me as if I was crazy. They must have thought, *ah, here it is – after these four years, she has finally gone mad!* I wasn't mad, I just knew what they needed to give them a fighting chance.

'How in the world do you expect to get this for two children, when it is so hard to even get it for one child?' one person asked. It was a fair point, but I had never been one to accept poor odds in the past. I wrote to a coordinator on a website and told them all about the AVT we had been doing at Oxford. Within an hour they were back in touch and said that they thought I could achieve this, and that they would send me someone who would assist through the whole process. It was overwhelming because this was the moment I knew my boys would be away from me for so long. They would be at school every weekday if this worked out – after four years of talking, reading, interacting constantly, someone else would be there, *many* other people would be there. The school said they were ready to begin, the therapists all agreed, but I felt the pressure. Ale said, 'If you think they are not ready, we'll wait six months.' I couldn't delay it though – this was the right thing for them.

The period before school was terrible. I couldn't sleep and I felt like crying in the park some days. How would I deal with school? How would I deal with the other parents? I wanted my kids to be seen as the same but I could not change the world. A very professional application was put together for each of the boys and we sent it in to our choice of school, knowing that it would take ninety days to find out if we had been successful. When I was told that it had been granted, that we had places for them both with Education Health and Care Plans (EHCPs) in place, I was so relieved. We had done it – everyone had pulled together and the impossible had been achieved. These plans would follow them for fifteen years and ensure full support, as well as a teaching assistant to be with them in class. The TA is very important as she will check that everything is OK and that they can hear. The plan would be reviewed every year and the boys would also be asked how they felt about their achievements and hopes. They would be involved in every aspect and that was a vital component of, ultimately, giving them agency over their own lives.

If you get the wrong person when you are at any point in this journey, or you're scared of the system, or you're not driven, then you're lost. And so are your kids. Mothers and fathers create the destiny of their children. Fear of the system can stop so many people; the wrong doctor, or nurse, or specialist can crush you. I have often asked myself, *what kept you going, Deborah?* There were many things I guess. I had Alessandro – I could talk to him about anything, even if I was exhausted. I was driven by the thought of the future for my boys, what it would be like if I left them in the land of the deaf. I had Keisha – I needed to give them the same options as her, but I also needed to give her a life that wasn't determined by people defining her by her poor, deaf brothers. I needed to get them into mainstream school. All of those things kept me going and they also taught me I was stronger than I had ever known, but I wouldn't want anyone to think that they are failing if they don't act in the same way because, the truth is, I struggled at times too.

I would say to Ale in the night, 'I am so tired – how do I do this? How do I deal with three kids and everything they need?' I had to hold myself together as I had to be there for all of them, and for my mamma, who could not be allowed to see me crumble, who could not deal with another blow in her life. My babbo would have been crazy for my kids and proud of me, and that kept me going. When he died, Mamma had moved to Milano to be with my sister as she was completely lost without Babbo. I knew she had this burden and I couldn't add to it, but I missed him too. From the moment the twins were born, to this day, I told them all about my father because I wanted him to be alive in their memories. I would have had a very different experience in Italy with the kids, but I so wish that he had been here to meet them all.

On the day Dylan and Zack went to school, my heart was bursting with pride. They were only four, such tiny boys, with their cochlears so obvious, and I tried to hide my worry they would be picked on as much as I could manage. They were the youngest in the class, standing there with their Spiderman and

Batman backpacks, wearing their little ties, school jumpers, shirts, and shorts with their white skinny legs poking out. They were happy knowing they would be with other kids, as I think they were bored of me by now! It was also Keisha's first day at that school as she had moved there so that they were all in the same place. As always, her understanding astounded me. I believe she sensed my anxiety so clearly, my worry that Zack and Dylan were being sent out into the world. As they all stepped through the school gate, she looked at me, smiled her wise little smile, and took each of them by the hand. It is like a photograph in my mind to this day. My three babies, all together, the twins' big sister protecting them and entering the playground as if to say, 'Here we are – watch out!' It was as if she was saying it would all be fine, that she would look after them for her mamma. It is a moment I will never forget. I was so proud, so very proud.

All I could think was, *wow, we have reached this point at last.* When they were born, I had been terrified of low expectations - I could only have dreamed of this. I was scared about the kind of school they could have gone to or the kind of friends they could have made, or even the academic skills they might have reached. Everything was a question mark in my mind but, in that moment, they couldn't know how proud they should be of themselves. They were scared - I knew that - but they were excited too, and they got strength from each other. A great teacher came out to welcome us that day and I will never forget her kindness; it helped to completely reframe how I felt about my boys going off onto their next adventure. Some parents were staring at Dylan and Zack, but one mother came over to chat and that was also a very uplifting thing to happen. People should know that the tiniest of gestures can make the biggest of differences, and never to hesitate if they feel they can offer a kindness. I think that those who stared simply did not recognise diversity and they didn't know how to react. The fact that some simply went with their hearts meant a great deal.

When I left the playground and went home, I counted the minutes until I could pick them up again; it was only a couple of hours for that first day but I'd never been away from them before. I was worried about everything – what if someone pushed one of them, what if the cochlear got broken, what if they were bullied, what if someone laughed at them? My mind could not settle but I knew it had to be done, and that I had brave, strong children.

I sat at my computer, but really I just floated until 11am. I know there was an issue there of losing control, of handing them over to strangers, and I was so anxious. They were without protection. I wasn't there to look after them as I'd always been up until this point. Ale was at work. He told me to relax but my biggest concern was that they would be in the playground at some point. That seemed like a wild, uncontrollable place. Naturally, I went to pick them up much earlier than I needed to, but when they came out they were both smiling and so happy.

'We are like Keisha now!' said Zack.

Their teacher was with them and she told me that it had all gone very well. After being shy at the beginning, they'd played well with all of the other pupils.

'We'll be doing an assessment in the next few days on all the kids,' she told me, and my heart sank. More assessments. As I stood talking to her, I was aware of the other parents collecting their children, but also watching us. I could see people staring at the cochlears and I was almost destroyed by thinking they saw them as the poor 'disabled' kids of the class.

'Are you sure they're thinking that or is it just you?' Ale asked when I cried that night. It was partly in my mind, as these people had never come across such a thing before, and it was something I had seen when at the park or in the street. After a few days, the head teacher said in reception, 'Zack and Dylan, welcome to our school. We are so happy to have you here!' That made me happy too!

When Dylan and Zack started mainstream school, I felt that I could finally breathe. We had come so far and it was a moment I had sometimes thought we would never see. We had all achieved this - our whole family and the wonderful team of doctors and specialists who had been beside us from the start.

It was not all perfect - for the first six months Dylan and Zack were so slow and tired. School was a shock for them and I was horrified at how they were achieving so little. They'd never been to nursery as we were told the environment wouldn't help them, so they'd had no prior experience of being in a similar environment. We actually thought we'd made the wrong choice for a while, but I had to hope that it would be fine. There is still low awareness of the new generation of CI kids. At the start of school, there was also the stress of people in general who kept staring at our kids in the park, on the streets, on planes, everywhere. This is one of the most painful moments for parents whose children have special needs, and I definitely had to work on it. I had to learn how to walk without seeing people's faces. Very few people had seen cochlears before, so my children had that to contend with too. People are desperate to fit in and often parents are in denial about anything to do with their children. When you deny things, the kids stay where they are. Denial often comes from shame, because we live in a world that values perfection. For people in general who were shocked or didn't know what to do when dealing with Dylan and Zack, I felt pity, because they are elevating perfection above all else and denying the beauty of difference to their own children. Some people think we should hide the cochlear by growing their hair, or they often wrongly believe that they are training aids which we hope will make them hear one day. You have to start conversations with people to challenge their prejudice or they will always think these things – that doesn't mean your heart doesn't sink when you see such prejudice being applied to your child. Just because my child does not look like your child, or act like your child, it doesn't mean he doesn't have feelings. If we all teach our children that we are all the same then that's the start of a better world.

I have also seen this with regards to adoption. One of the things that disappoints parents of adopted or special needs children, is the curiosity and staring from other parents or children. No matter where you come from, you are family, and it is sad that some people never understand that. It was always something we faced head on from the beginning. I never considered breast feeding Zack and Dylan as I hadn't fed Keisha. When I was pregnant, I didn't want to show my tummy or talk about it, as I didn't want to hurt Keisha or exclude her. As I have said, we chose American names for the boys rather than Italian, or they would have been Paolo and Ricardo. We have never created a difference and we tell other people to ensure they don't either. A child is a child.

Now that the boys were getting older, and their hearing with the implants was so good, it was vitally important to use the right words, to set the right tone and environment for all of them. Children pick up on the slightest nuance, and being cautious about ever bringing negativity into their lives through how you talk and interact with others has such an effect. Keisha always says that she is very lucky – she sees her extended family as lucky, not something to make her sad. Why would she be sad? She has more people in her life and she will be the most extraordinary person. Of course, there may be wobbles as she turns into a teenager, but we don't know what they will be or when they will happen. We will deal with it just like we deal with everything, just like every parent chooses their way to deal with things. If you give a positive approach, your children have that. If you hide, that causes problems. Life is ongoing and we sort things as they come. People have fixed ideas of what makes a family, but the world is changing –

rightly so. We've made our family work because DNA doesn't really matter. It matters how little ones grow with you. None of my children are genetically connected to me in any way but they all have so much in common with me. They are mine and I am theirs; how it all started means nothing when you consider it that way.

Sadly, not everyone has this approach. It is very hard to cope with intrusive and pitiful looks. This is the first psychological hurdle parents of 'special' children need to overcome. In the most severe instances, it can take the shape of pure discrimination. On holiday, I once heard a mum telling her child to go and play somewhere away from Dylan and Zack. Another woman stopped me on the beach and asked me why my daughter was with me given that her skin colour was different from mine. Another told her children to keep their distance from my twins because they had a rare illness.

Whilst you are tempted to remain speechless in these circumstances, I choose to talk, explain, educate. Things will get better in the future, but only with a different education that needs to happen at school and within families. Be strong and do not take it personally. After all, life has given you and your children the opportunity to grow without prejudice, which is a privilege. Some days will always be difficult, but look ahead, keeping a driven and positive attitude.

I wasn't only having to face challenging attitudes from some people when we moved here, but also the growing realisation that Alessandro was unhappy. He had moved into a different section of the company when we moved to England, and he hated it. It was a completely different culture and he felt that his career was over. He was so bored. His mind started a train of negative thoughts as a result of the shock to his system of being in another part of the company where there was no drive, no commitment. I had what I wanted, and I knew that the progress of all our children was on the trajectory I had dreamed of – the boys would have therapy and a state school, and we would all have a normal life. At times, normal was an achievement I could only pray for, but it was coming to fruition. It was not the same for Ale. Yes, he was around more and more for a relationship with the children, which he loved, but a huge part of him had been taken away by the move. He was very low. I should have seen it coming when he had a complete burnout.

I was holding everything together again, and school was not as smooth as I had hoped it would be at this stage. I think, at times, I was in shock. It is tough for any mamma when their baby starts school, and I felt that I had been thrown into a completely different world – again. When I saw that the twins were not coming on as quickly as they should, my anxiety started to creep in once more. On one of our appointments, I asked what I should do given that Zack and Dylan were struggling, tired, and so behind during their first six months.

'They are just little,' I was told. 'Still babies really as they have been through so much. Are you using the FM system?'

We were not as this was something that took longer through the SENCO, and the FM actually only arrived six months after the boys started school. A frequency modulation system is a wireless assistive hearing device that enhances what cochlear implants can do, especially when the wearers are in noisy or busy environments, such as classrooms or schools. They work by being able to pick up sound closer to its source, or they can be connected directly to the sound source and transmitted more clearly alongside a reduction in background noise. It was something we needed to fight for.

'What are you doing at weekends?' the doctor asked me.

'Everything!' I excitedly told him. 'We do so much!

'Well, don't. Let them sleep, don't try to stimulate them as they'll be tired. Get them to bed at 7pm every night and don't let them stay up later on the weekend. Let them rest from their week and don't expect that they won't be exhausted.' This was a revelation to me. I always felt the pressure of expectations, even when they were mine alone, which had made me so frustrated when the twins weren't reading and writing, but everything changed within about two months and they started hitting all of their targets. There were two reasons for this – one was the increased amount of sleep they were having in order to recover from their busy week, the second was when we changed to the new processor which cut back on background noise.

Therapy teaches deaf children how to hear, but there also has to be a consideration of how they hear through the cochlear as this is different to how the hearing of someone with no deafness processes sound. I think what we can all learn from that is that each of us would benefit from looking at how we process what seems perfectly natural to us. It is so important to pay attention to what other people are telling you. If the school had not informed me that Zack and Dylan were falling behind, I would not have been able to act. The problem is that many parents have a kneejerk response when they are told anything about their child that they perceive as negative.

Your child is being disruptive.

No! That can't be true – it must be another child who sits next to them.

Your child can't concentrate.

Not my son! He concentrates very well at home – is it a new teacher perhaps?

Your child is falling behind.

That can't be the case – my daughter is very clever; all of the family say this.

Open your ears – listen. They are telling you these things for a reason. If your child is on computer games or watching TV for hours, it will affect their sleep and that will affect their concentration. If you don't have boundaries for your child, it will impact on their behaviour. If you do not focus on their ability, they will never know what they can achieve, so may get frustrated. Teachers don't point these things out for fun and they don't lie – they tell you so that you can stop the train and get it back on the right track. Stop for one second and accept that they are telling you for a reason.

Of course, not everything is set in stone, not everything we are told is right is actually good for us. However, don't confuse these two things. As a parent, you need to recognise what is good, appropriate advice and what is actually not in line with what will be the best future for everyone. For you, for your children, for everyone in your life, every morning you have two choices: continue to sleep with your dreams or wake up and chase them.

I realised from this point on that everything I had learned, and everything I would apply to my life forever, could all be reduced to that one question. Sleeping with your dreams or chasing them - which one are you choosing today?

CHAPTER SEVENTEEN
MY WORLD

In July 2017, we received the amendments to Zack and Dylan's Education Health & Care Plans, which were formulated after their Annual Review Meetings. In amongst the pages of official documentation, I could see my boys. I could see their personalities and their wonderful little lives opening out in front of me. Each of them had written a profile page which meant more than all the forms in the world.

Zack had written:

I am always happy and smiling.
I love playing with my brother Dylan, my sister and my friends.
I listen hard, am curious about everything and am a good learner.
I am a good singer, am good at puzzles and have a good imagination.
I always try my best with the learning the class is doing.

The best way to support me is:
To always have my cochlear implants on.
I love reading books and telling stories.

To be good at things.
I love to respect rules.
I like playing with my friends.
I like going swimming
I like eating pancakes!
I like going on holiday and going skiing.

In his review was a summary of his life so far – the plan is described as one for 'education, health and care' but it can be a little unsettling to see your child's life described so starkly, written down in the words of professionals:

'Zack is one of twins who were born in New York to Italian parents. The family moved to the UK in May 2013 having previously lived in Mexico City since the twins were one year old. He also has an older sister. He has a congenital, profound hearing loss. He underwent surgery for bilateral cochlear implants at the age of six months and has received habilitation using the Auditory Verbal approach since seven months of age.

'Zack hears English and Italian as spoken language and is able to understand and speak both languages fluently. Deborah praises the cochlear implant technology and practitioners that have enabled Zack, and his twin brother Dylan, to hear when they are profoundly deaf. Zack is totally reliant on his hearing technology and does not hear in the same way that a hearing child would.

'Deborah has worked extremely hard to ensure Zack is bilingual and able to engage fully in the hearing world. Zack has worked hard at Auditory Verbal Therapy training, ensuring that his speech and language is in line with his peers. Deborah understands what support Zack needs within his mainstream classroom to enable him to have equal learning opportunities. Zack is very aware if his cochlear comes loose and will immediately say if he cannot hear.

'Mum describes Zack as a 'clever boy' and as sensitive, can be emotional, and is a perfectionist. He loves school and does not tolerate getting things wrong. Zack is not so confident with people until he has got to know them. Zack does have some difficulties with balance, but he is now taking part in more sporting activities and doing well.

'Mum describes Dylan as a 'smart boy' and the 'engineer' of the family. She says he is willing to 'have a go' and to speak up and give answers to adult questions straight away, without fear of being wrong.

'Deborah would like Zack to have further opportunities to focus on 'Theory of Mind' (what other people are thinking). AVT are also now focusing on thinking independently – having strategies to work things out. Deborah wants Zack to be accepting of his cochlear as he grows older, to be able to confidently and clearly explain their value, and to look after them independently. They already practice independence with the cochlear at home.

'In line with AVT, Zack's parents have high aspirations for him; they want him to always believe 'I can' and that he can reach any goals. They say their wish for Zack is to reach his full potential and for him to be able to listen, and speak, and access the curriculum alongside his hearing peers. They would like all professionals working with Zack to liaise with and engage in his AVT.'

Dylan had written:

I am always happy, easy going and love fun!
I love playing with my brother, Zack, my sister and my friends.
I enjoy learning, am curious and a hard worker.
I love being independent in everything.
I am good at helping other people in the class.
The best way to support me is:
To always have my cochlear implants on.
I like to go to the toy shop.
I like to go to the park.
I like tennis and swimming.

I like trying new things.
I like looking after new children.
I like going skiing and going on holiday with my family.
My friends and family.
I like playing outside with my friends at school.

They both had the same comments to encourage people to support them:

If I cannot hear, please check my cochlear. If it is not working, call my mum immediately.
Be normal with me as you would hearing children.
Allow me to sit close to the teacher during lessons.
Repeat instructions if the room is noisy.
Do not sit me close to the window or in very noisy situations.
Wait and give me time to answer.
Encourage me with sports to improve my balance.
Make sure my implants do not get wet or sandy or hit by balls.
Let me play when I am tired.
Encourage me to 'have a go'!

Use the digital radio wherever possible in the school.

They had been asked what their hopes and dreams were for their futures, and the boys had each written:

I will be a brilliant and hard-working student.
I will be independent, including with my cochlear, and able to explain my cochlear to others.
I will extend my friendships and be part of a sports team.

The plans had always recognised the need for a good listening environment for the boys, and that support needed to be flexible to meet their needs at given times, to encourage their independence and inclusion at other times. They need appropriate listening conditions and they need additional support in noisier environments. *Children who have a hearing loss who are using cochlear implants can tire quickly as a result of the effort of listening in a busy classroom and often need language/instructions reinforced individually or in small groups*, said the report. I was so glad they contextualised everything, recognising how the research applied to the twins, and yet still giving them the power to speak about what they needed. It was such a touching moment to read those documents, and one of reflection too.

It is very hard indeed to keep a sense of yourself in the middle of such family challenges like ours. Some people go through much worse, while some people go through nothing at all. For me, I had to do these things, I had to fight for my boys, but I lost myself for a while. There was a niggle in my mind after some time which was taking me back to my past, when I had a career, when I thought I would always know what to do in life. When I pulled that thread, I could see that it was all linked to my homeland, to the way things are done there. In Italy, politicians in particular talk, talk, talk. Although I had thought for some time that my future would be in politics, in diplomacy, I had soon realised that I like to act, I like to get things done. Italy is a static country, not enough gets done. This is why I had loved marketing – marketing is action. It was also why I had loved New York, before things changed for us. I don't like to waste time, and while I would never think that I had wasted time giving my children as much as I could, I had spent very little on me.

I felt my brain was soft. I had no inspiration and it made me feel desperate. The kids had needed me for so long but now they were flying. I was not deluding myself; I have a six-year gap in my CV and there are younger people out there hustling for jobs that no one would consider me for. The truth was, even shops wouldn't accept me as an assistant. I was too old, too out of touch with everything. What would I do?

I thought I knew what had to be done, what I needed to do to get Deborah back, but I wasn't acting on it until that point. If you don't act on it, you will never achieve your dream. In one afternoon, I listed actions, things I needed to do – I would write a book, study on a life coaching course, set up a website to present myself as a life coach, and start setting deadlines.

Over six years, I lost me.

Alessandro always encouraged me, always saying that I needed to become alive again. I needed to create a job for me. I needed to invest in me. I wanted my daughter to see me work and I wanted to help people with what I had learned in the past six years. People think less of you when you are always at home with your children, I really think they do, but I had no time to work, just as they had no time to find out what my story was.

From the moment I had been told that kids who spend the first three or four years with someone working so hard on them when there is brain plasticity, that they are the ones you can tell will have a fighting chance, was it for me. My own brain switched immediately and I knew they would always be my priority. Now, however, now they would benefit from a mamma who was taking time to make her mark on the world again. I had spent so many days talking, reading, going to the park, going to the supermarket, just on them and their needs. I had no time to lose – this was their future. But I had spent no time on me so I had lost my future. Six years out for a 45-year-old is very different to when she is 25 or 35. I became another person. I was not carefree anymore and I thought I'd never come back again. Mums of kids with disabilities lose their freedom and I needed to reclaim something of mine.

Things started to fall into place. I discovered that an American woman who was now living in Tuscany had established a huge community on hearing loss. This woman – Jodi Cutler – had been told by her newborn son's paediatrician in the USA that she was neurotic after repeatedly expressing her concerns that her baby was not hearing properly. 'There is nothing wrong with him,' she was told. 'You need to stop being so anxious.' It is so often the way. So often the mamma is told that *she* is the problem instead of being taken seriously. When her son was born there was no Early Hearing Detection Intervention program, and only after the family moved to Italy did their new pediatrician truly listen to her concerns.

Jodi's son Jordan was diagnosed with profound bilateral neurosensorial hearing loss at twelve months of age, in Florence, in 1997. He immediately received hearing aids, and at eight years of age received his first cochlear implant, in Pisa. Jodi says that Italy saved their lives.

It varies for everyone; we were so lucky in NYC but every parent has a different experience because it all depends on the doctor you find. I felt that New York gave us incredible doctors, whereas Jodi felt they dismissed and patronised her.

Jodi's experience led her to set up a website for parents of children with hearing loss, and that is how I found her. I sent her an email telling her of our experience and she replied immediately.

This is the best email I have ever received in my life, she wrote. *I want to present you to my forum . . . and I would love if you would consider becoming an administrator of it too.*

It was such a wonderful opportunity! Jodi invited me to a Parliamentary conference in Rome and it was such a revelation. Not only could I speak, but people wanted to listen. Parents, audiologists, speech therapists – all of them gave me the proof that this was a moment for me. I discovered a world of kindness that she had built which opened up my passion for the world I had felt excluded from for so long. I could see how many incredible people, how many incredible parents, existed and how we could meet and support each other through social media. Jodi was an icon for me because she was there for so many families, even with just the right word at the right time. I learned so much from her that informs my life and I would never have met her without this experience.

'I think I know what to do,' I said to Jodi. 'I have been thinking for a while about where my journey will take me next and I want to be a life coach. It must be for those who have children with special needs, and for women seeking the resources necessary to live meaningful, fulfilled lives.' It was through Jodi that I learned the importance of being passionate about something. She is one of the best people I have ever met and she has given me so much. From her website, I also learned how important it is to have family support in this situation. I was never part of a forum and I discovered it thanks to her. Even sharing experiences would have made me less anxious in the early days. At that point, I decided to open a forum for Italian families called 'AViTalia' which would help many to get information about this extraordinary therapy we had accessed all around the world, and which had given our kids the wings to fly.

I began my coaching studies in London and Milan, knowing from the start that this was what I needed to do at this point in my life. I'd always worked at a high level, I'd always been ambitious, and then I had done nothing but therapy and hospitals for so long. I had been lost in a world that didn't belong to me. When we came to the UK, I was a housewife and I had no wish to take that role, however, it had been what I needed to do at that point. The twins were not the same as other kids, I just couldn't give up. I couldn't work twelve-hour days in a new career or go back to my old one; life had changed me, and I had to embrace it. Now? Now was the next chapter.

My children were the only reason I would ever have given up my career - for their future. I had always thought I'd go back to work one day, go back to being me. Yes, I could have paid other people, but I needed to be there for them. The doctors always told me they would not have reached this level without me. If they had gone to daycare at six months old with forty other kids, even in the best daycare, they would have fallen so far behind that they could never have been brought back. Deciding not to go back to work was the toughest decision of my life. I was ambitious, but I needed to transfer that ambition to my kids. I needed to create something for myself. I needed to be successful.

Everything had been done in stages, but it had all built up into a full picture. When the EHC plans came into place, I felt as if they were covered for the next fifteen years of their lives and there was such relief. However, there are always administrative hoops to jump through when you have a SEN child. The administration fills your life. HECP and DLA are not just simple documents to complete, they are worrying and time-consuming, they have a great deal of negative impact in the family and add to the stress of the diagnosis, but you need to fight to get them and have the best support for your kids.

The impact of a diagnosis like this on the family life is widespread, that can't be denied. We travel as much as we can on holiday, but our dreams to actually live in other countries can't be realised for a long time. I want to travel but they need to stay here. Spain, France, Portugal would be no good for them. Here, if I have problems with the cochlear, I send it away and it's back in twenty-four hours. Unless you have seen the difference these implants make, you cannot understand how they change lives. That Dylan and Zack speak fluent English and Italian, and are learning more languages, bewilders many people.

You have to remember that everything can be positive – the things which happen to you, which you didn't want, which you didn't ask for, can be the very things which you need. Your children's voice will be what you teach them. If that voice is constantly negative and all about what they can't do, then they will only see restrictions and darkness. Yes, our family struggled, there is no doubt about that, but we have worked constantly to give our children the best possible future. You have to focus on their abilities and let them know they can cherish their diversity. They are who they are, and the world should not expect them to change unless they want it.

Zack recently wrote a letter to the Tooth Fairy. In it, he said: *Dear fairy, please leave me some money for an ice cream, but please don't take my tooth. It's the first tooth I've lost, and I would like to keep it all my life. Tomorrow, maybe even a second one will fall.* Then he asked Ale and me to put the cochlear close to him, so that if the fairy wanted to talk to him he could immediately put it on for their conversation.

'Mum, does the Tooth Fairy have cochlear?' he wanted to know . . . and those are the moments when you know everything has all worked out. Last year, we went back to New York and the kids were playing in Central Park with other children. One little American boy said to Zack, 'Are you Harry Potter, because you speak just like him?' It was so funny for us all, but it also made us realise how important all of the choices have been as they have pushed them to reach their goals. The boy did not ask Zack anything about his diversity, only about his lovely British accent!

Our boys have developed into such wonderful characters. Zack sleeps like a buddha and smiles as he dreams. Dylan is a screamer and lies all scrunched up until morning. They have been different since the moment they were born, and I know they will achieve anything they set their minds to.

It's not a matter of thinking out of the box – it's realising there is *no* box. When we overcome our self-limiting beliefs, we can feel really free. In that moment we can reach any goal! Our beliefs may not exist in our minds as explicit propositions; they may be so implicit in our thinking that we are hardly aware of them at all, for they lie behind our actions. If I say, 'I'm powerless about this situation,' it means I will never stand up and change things. If I identify the limiting belief and I work on it trying to understand where it comes from, I can challenge it. Once I challenge it, I can say, 'I can do something!'

Just because you are a parent, does not mean that you can't also be your child's coach. Each of us has our own confidence level; for some children it comes naturally, whilst for others it needs to be practised. Feeling the trust from your parents and educators are crucial pillars. Constant training on many fronts is essential, as is encouragement to get out of comfort zones. Positivity, confidence and persistence are key in life, so never give up on yourself or your children.

If we spend a lot of our energy worrying about things that we can't control, we end up feeling powerless and overwhelmed. We need to focus our energy on the areas we can control.

Try it.

Don't stop until you are proud.

I always say, 'If you are the most interesting person in the room, you are in the wrong room!' We went through so much, I have lines on my face, I have become another person, but as a life coach for parents with a child with disabilities, I can empower people. Whatever you do, don't dream of winning. Train yourself to actually win. Train your children to think about strategies to win, to question themselves, to understand what is holding them back – then do the same with yourself.

Women are so strong emotionally. I had to do it all as we needed Ale's job, which gave me no choice. In the beginning he was in another country, listening to me on the phone, crying and desperate, then Googling. For the first eight months I was alone.

There was so much pressure and I also had to keep the pressure off him as much as possible. Friends would moan about potty training and I'd think, *you don't know what problems are.* I looked back and wondered whether there were things that I hadn't dealt with the way I should, whether they were still dragging me down. If you want to become a coach, you have to be coached; from this, I realised that when I was battling against infertility, I was constantly tormented by the question, *why me?* Thanks to my coach I was able to park this question that didn't take me anywhere and ask myself other, more useful questions: *What could I learn from this situation? What skills can I use to deal with this situation?*

Questions like that help you to move on rather than keeping you in a bad place. Each level of your life will demand a different you, so all you can do is focus on what is in front of you each day. What if I told you that in ten years your life would be the same as today, the only thing that would have changed is that you would be ten years older? Why are you so afraid of change? Strength is within you; no one else can give you that or do it for you. You have to do it yourself. There are opportunities even in the most difficult moments. Calm down and see what the opportunity is and just think about this. The real opportunity for me through all of this has been the chance to reinvent myself. I would never have done it otherwise.

We will never know how many people give up just when they are on the brink of success. We will never know how many people would have learned from their failures because they decide it is too much of a fight. If we all make a commitment to focus on the abilities of our children, we can change that in a generation.

Let's teach our children to listen to other children and to respect their turn, don't bully, don't push in, learn from everyone no matter how small their contribution may be. From listening to the story of another child, our children can learn about them and their thoughts. Let's tell our children about their friends' cultures so they can develop their own opinion and not prejudices. Let's teach them how important it is to be curious about other cultures and why they make our world a better place.

If our child comes home telling us about another child they have seen who looked lonely or was experiencing a problem, let's stimulate our child to get close and be of help. If a child is alone at the playground or at school, we can tell our children to go and invite them to join in their play. Let's stimulate our children to integrate newcomers, let's make an effort to introduce ourselves to new families so they feel welcome and included and we set a good example. If we know about a child who has different abilities, we can teach our children to be inclusive with this child. It is normal to ask questions about diversity (children are naturally curious), but teaching them that diversity is an asset and not a liability is of paramount importance.

As adults too, we all tend to judge and quickly jump to conclusions. It is hard to monitor our thoughts and feelings but we need to stop, breathe, reflect and ask ourselves questions that allow us to be better people. Teaching children about empathy teaches us to become more empathetic, and we can all prevent bullying or indifference from developing during adolescence. Let's make an effort together. Our children are worth it – we're all worth it.

CHAPTER EIGHTEEN
LESSONS FOR LIFE

As a mum of children with special needs, I have adopted specific strategies to cope with the prying looks my boys sometimes get when we are out and about, at the park, in the street, on holiday – everywhere really. 'The looks' are a reason for anxiety and pain for mammas. I understand that perfectly. You spot people doing 'the look' and feel hurt, especially when you realise that often 'the looks' are coming from the same people. Whilst we all understand that we cannot change other people, we can change the way we react to those people's actions and the way we see the world. I cannot do anything about people who stare at my children with the weird things coming out of their heads, but I can change how to react to them and even choose not to react at all.

I try and hang out with people who are open and have a positive attitude. I refrain from paying too much attention when I see we are observed. I listen to my music, take a deep breath and say 'Hi' to everybody with a big smile on my face. I greet the boys and start my day with optimism because I refuse to let myself get dragged down by people with closed or narrow attitudes. Move on when you come across people like that, and don't be too disappointed as there will always be more of them. Work on your mind as much as you can and build a network of inspiring and supportive people. Ultimately, it is about being proud of the difference your children have, the thing that makes them unique and special. Your children will feel this too and learn to be proud of who they are. Don't let them see any negativity from you or they will wonder if it is their fault. A positive attitude will be contagious and spread out to other parents, for example, which will then have a ripple effect to their children who will be more open to involving children with differences.

Cultivating our open-mindedness and passing it on to our children is the greatest gift we can give them, and an investment in their future. Why would you choose not to give them something so wonderful and free? I recently had an annual check for Zack and Dylan's hearing and implant.

Once in the waiting room, I noticed a couple of young parents waiting, possibly for the hearing screening of their newborn baby. Chances were that the little one had not passed the hearing test at birth and they might have been there for a repeat of the test. I could spot concern on their faces about what the diagnoses could be. We then saw them being called by the doctors and we got called in right after them. Once I got out with Zack and Dylan, I spotted the father again and he was in tears. The woman looked petrified. That was the same grief I experienced six years before. I could feel their pain and, for a moment, I was taken back in time.

We got closer to the family and Zack asked me, 'Mamma, why are these people crying?' This was the first time I had found myself in this situation so I told Zack that the parents were sad because their little one couldn't hear.

Zack's reaction was extraordinary. 'What is the problem, Mum? We hear more than you do.'

The couple heard this and saw Zack with his cochlear and I believe I saw relief wash over them as they saw possibilities ahead.

The diagnosis stage is a very difficult one to accept and there is definitely grief involved at that moment. Nonetheless, there is also light, there is hope. The best thing to do is to be pragmatic, understand what is possible and make a clear action plan. It is important to accept the reality you have in front of you; avoid denial as it will only hold you back. With organisation and optimism, extraordinary results can be achieved. Yes, it is hard work almost every moment of every day, but there will be the most incredible results from your commitment. Trust your instinct, trust your child's potential, and the unthinkable will materialise in front of you.

When I was trying to find my way to a family, it was so important I let Alessandro see who I was – it was then I realised that being honest in a relationship means the other person can choose whether they want to be with the authentic you, or a version which is not the real you. That, as I have said, was the point where I knew it was better to be alone than to be with someone who did not appreciate who you were and what you wanted in life. I now also see that as a mother. My children have a wonderful approach to life. Recently, they read *Jonathan Livingston Seagull*, the delightful story of a little bird who wants to fly for the simple reason that he has a passion for it. They related to it so much, as they know that one of the worst things they could ever do was to just copy others in order to fit in.

It matters that children believe these words from that wonderful book:

Don't believe what your eyes are telling you. All they show is limitation. Look with your understanding. Find out what you already know and you will see the way to fly.

Everyone needs to know their own mind – if you learn it in childhood then you can apply it all of your life. What greater gift could a parent give their child?

I was so lucky that I had a wonderful childhood and, looking back, I think that even the things which were difficult helped to make me who I am today. When I went through my illness, when I had to deal with my own disfigurement, all of it contributed to making me strong. If your child is also going through things which are a challenge, keep your tears for when they cannot see you – not for everything, but for any heartache you feel about them and what they are going through. Cry at films together, cry at beautiful music and incredible art, show them that there is nothing to be ashamed of in emotion, but never make them think they are causing you upset. They need to see you be strong for them so they can learn to be that way too. If your child ever says to you, 'I can't do this,' work through it with them. Find solutions, don't let them give up, but show them how to reach that point. It is as the old quote says, *give a man a fish, and you feed him for a day; teach a man to fish, and you feed him for a lifetime*. Every child has such potential and it really is everyone's duty to do all they can to help them reach the heights they deserve. They deserve the world.

It is not a walk in the park, but if you work their voice will be what you teach them. You must have a positive attitude, especially in front of your children. We are not superheroes, we are normal people, but once we had the boys I knew we had four years to give them the strength to be who they are now. There were so many problems – our relationship, the fact that we had to work morning to evening on different things, but they never saw the despair. You can struggle, but there is always hope. There are limits but pay attention to your kids, show them passion and positivity, and they will shine. If they are put in a corner, they will stay there. We always thought the twins could do it, and now they do.

I believe that if you want to be great and successful, choose people who are great and successful to be with you, and walk side by side with them. They need to be a good example for you. Follow them. Meet them and work with them. When I reached the bottom with various problems I had in life, I always tried to go on with strength. I always read a lot and I always looked to people who could teach me, people who inspired me. In my case they were almost all women, and thanks to them I have changed and managed to recreate a life for myself. They didn't necessarily help me directly but I listened to them every day. They were my heroines and they believed in me and my children, always pushing them up and never labelling them as 'less'. Terri, Lilian, Susie, Mrs Elliot and Mrs Rigby - who are the teachers of the twins - were all incredible, and many of them continue to be, letting the boys be independent and also telling me to step back when I need to!

I questioned myself once I studied how they had dealt with things and how they had moved through life. The people you learn from are not necessarily your best friends; they must be people who question and challenge you. They can't be people who approve of everything you do, no matter what. Surround yourself with people who have reacted to what life has thrown at them, who have made breakthroughs. Don't take their hands, don't rely on them to make your decisions for you, but walk near them to figure out how to act. They are, and will be, examples for you.

Remember Galileo Galilei said, 'You can't teach anybody anything, only make them realise the answers are already inside them.' You have the answer. No one else. But you have to be close to people or surrounded by people who will challenge you. Zack and Dylan inspire us and challenge us because they had such a tough start at the beginning of their life, but they used all of their abilities to reach the level of their peers. They work hard and they always smile. They are proud of who they are. They try every single day to reach a new goal and when they reach it, it's like they are touching the sky. They never take anything for granted and I can still learn from that, even though I am their mother, even though I am the grown up. The beginning of everything is in your imagination, and working hard, focusing on your goals, and really believing that you can do it, is how to turn it into reality.

As I have written this book, I have gone back and checked with Alessandro whether dates are right, whether times are right but, actually, none of that really matters. The important things are that we got through and that all three of our children are wonderful people. Ale told me that he has regrets from the time at the beginning, when I had the obsession and he was in Mexico most of the time. He sees that as the moment when our crisis was at the highest peak and feels that he went the other way. He believes he lost perspective and forgot to focus on what was important.

'I could have supported you better,' he told me. 'I could have been more thoughtful. Maybe I added to the problems. I felt as far as the cochlear and everything to do with deafness was concerned, you were in charge and I was an observer on the sidelines. I should have been more involved. The therapy became a Deborah thing and I should have played more of a part. You made it a mission and I felt you thought all of it was your fault. The reality is that we don't know and you are the best mamma in the world, so how could anything be your fault?' I think he was just starting to rethink his life and rethink the way he was living. Ale wanted to have time with us, to find time for us. He was not realising in that moment that, thanks to all the problems we had, he was actually making huge breakthroughs as a man, as a manager. We had no choice in the past about what we could do as we needed his job to give our kids the best future. Now it was time to start *our* future as we wanted it to be.

When I was a kid, my parents told me how important it was to have a 'regular' career - doctor, lawyer, accountant, engineer, teacher, professor were all perfect jobs in their minds. These were professions that would lead to a career for life - a job there would always be a need for and no one would kick you out of it. Then, once I graduated, I was told I needed many 'certifications' to show future employers. The more certifications you have, the better work will be for you. Then I started working in advertising and I thought it was the job of my life because I got a permanent contract. What a tiny thing to worry about! I grew up with the idea that I needed *un posto fisso* and I have often worked many hours a day thinking it was my only choice if I was to afford everything - vacations, mortgage, my potential family life, and to assure a safe future to my kids as my parents did for me. I was paid for eight hours a day and I thought it was better to work twelve hours per day. Why? Because I wanted to succeed in my career and keep my job forever.

But that was a long time ago. The world my parents grew up in is so far away from the world I live, and we all live, in now. I truly believe certifications mean little compared to experience. There are no lifelong careers anymore, in fact, many current jobs will not exist in ten years. We all need a passion for what we do, and that cannot be found simply by trying to work out what will be a job for life. We need to work out how high we can dream and recognise that the only limit is the sky. I would never have thought I would be where I am now, but if I had not faced such struggles, I would be in a place which wasn't right for me – in advertising, in marketing, never seeing my children, always chasing a higher pay cheque. I would never have thought I could be who I am now. As a coach, every day I meet extraordinary people, people who re-invented their life because their world changed. How lucky are we that we can follow our passions?

There is another aspect to what I now coach which has come directly from our experiences. What Alessandro said about perhaps not being there for us in the right way, and what his burnout taught us, is that sometimes men are left feeling outsiders in their own families. I passionately believe we need to address that.

When you undergo therapy for family issues, you are usually encouraged to involve *all* of the family. It is so important that fathers attend too, because when your child or children faces challenges, so does your relationship. It is easy to slip into very stereotypical roles, where the mother does everything relating to care, education and medical appointments, and the father sees himself as little more than the money earner. On top of this, I believe that women and men often approach problems with their children in a difficult way – whether that is because of nature or nurture can be something we debate forever, but I certainly feel (and see) that women tend to take on the emotional side of things, and men take on the work-based side of things (not necessarily what could be called the 'practical' side, as a woman dealing with doctors and appointments, with teachers and schools, is focused on all of that too). I believe it is absolutely vital that fathers have to be involved at all levels, and that mothers sometimes have to take a step back. It is so tempting, as a mamma, to think you have to do everything and that something will go wrong if you don't. A martyr complex helps no one, least of all your child, and you must – when you can – reclaim your life, step by step.

Both parents must be involved in child rearing whenever possible. Of course, couples separate, but that is no excuse for the father (or the mother in the rarer cases where she is the one who has left or does not have custody) to simply walk away from doing all they can to make their child's life as full as possible. There are benefits for the absent parents too if they know they have stepped up. It works for everyone. I am not denying there are some instances where a parent simply cannot be given access to the child because of safeguarding issues, but wherever possible do not desert your child just because your relationship has broken down. You loved them once, do not let that love die.

Children learn different things from mummies and daddies but it is too easy to not see that, which is why I started to work with men to say, 'This is what you need to think about as a father, as a man.' I developed the concept of 'Daddy as Coach' whereby men are encouraged to channel the aspects of them, which can benefit their children hugely.

It is so important to challenge gender stereotypes which do nothing but put our children into boxes – boxes which, as adults, can lead to abusive relationships, restricted ambition, and a fear of reaching for the stars. Let us encourage little girls to dream of being princesses who do sports and who work because they are smart, not as passive weaklings who are unable to make their own choices. Let's stop the idea of the princess waiting for Prince Charming without another role – they can still have all the accessories and play they want but give them the belief that they will be the women of the future too, the strong women, the leaders. Let us encourage little boys to be in touch with their feelings, to know they can show emotions. Let us tell them that if they become fathers, they will have an important input into the lives of their children and that they can be role models full of warmth and empathy, as well as strength and ambition. Our children all deserve this.

At night, when Dylan and Zack go to sleep, we charge the batteries of the cochlear and let the implant rest. When I turn on the charger, I think the day is over and I think of all the new information that came to my children, the new things they learned, the new feelings they felt. It is a time to reflect. It is as if everything is concentrated in those little lights as they charge. Every day, it is as if we have crossed a busy road, full of information charging down every highway. As we navigate it, our lives and minds are enriched, and this applies to adults as well as children. We all need to be recharged.

Those little lights signify so much – in them, I can read their actions, the actions of the days. I can't deny it: sometimes I cry because I think my life would have been easier without deafness, but then I immediately think of all the new conquests that the children have made. Of course, their failures are there, we all have a degree of that, but there are also their strategies, the way they face life with pride and determination. Through these lights I see how many wonderful things they have learned. Listening to their minds, three different trains of thought coming from our three children, fascinates me every day. So, on each of those days, I sit and write. I have done this every day for nine years. I note everything that has been beautiful and what they learned from the day, what they did wrong and what they should improve. They make mistakes just like any children (I am not saying they are perfect by any means!), but then they learn from mistakes and that is one of the best approaches to life at all stages, for everyone.

After I have written about my children's day, I do the same for me. I wonder what worked in my day as a parent and as a coach, what I could do better, then I read and study to improve. If you do this every night, it will take some time to understand what worked for your child and for you, in your work and your personal life, but it is definitely worth it. Write it down and you will be surprised to see how many things we take for granted and how you can actually make life strategies based on what has happened. Often there are patterns which we do not recognise – sometimes because we do not want to – and this process can help you understand so much about your life. Ask yourself this question: are you surrounding yourself with people who build you up or throw you down? Are you working towards a goal, or heading in the right direction? Or are you aimless and just accepting whatever life throws at you?

When I was told the twins could not hear, I would never have even imagined they could have achieved so much. Many children in the world have difficult beginnings and happiness needs to be fought for every single day but, believe me, every step is the greatest of successes. Always aim high for them, no one knows what their limit will be, so why restrict that before they have even started? Stimulate them and let them make mistakes because the further they fall, the further they rise. Children are not born to be perfect, but they must always have our trust.

To give them what they need, you need to find yourself. 'Difficult' doesn't mean 'impossible,' it simply means you have to work harder. Every day I meet extraordinary women who have such difficult lives but manage to remain strong. Their attitudes give me the motivation to work with them, to help them gain awareness about how many possibilities they have to improve their life situation, creating the change they need to overcome their traumas. All of them reflect on their story and discover an unexpected strength inside them, something they didn't think was there.

Nobody is born weak. We only learn to think of ourselves as weak individuals, but deep inside we have an amazing strength that just needs to be uncovered. When we reflect and cultivate our self-awareness, we rediscover this strength and make it a protagonist in our life. I remember my journey during the adoption process - once all the steps had been completed, I became really anxious and kept checking for new email, waiting for phone calls, desperate for the agency to get in touch. It pushed my mental balance completely out of touch, but I used work and activity to focus my energy elsewhere. When my OBGYN told me it would be impossible to conceive naturally, it was tough, but I accepted it. I had to wrestle with the negative emotions from those words, but I was motivated to see how I could get what I wanted – a family. The massive uncertainty surrounding the whole fertility process, the constant fear of failing, meant that I had to catch deep breaths to remain positive every day. I hated the waiting rooms at the clinic, but at the same time I forced myself to think that was the right course of action to achieve my dream to give Keisha siblings. And I succeeded. It wasn't easy, but it was that strength that helped me power through the process.

When I learned from the doctors that the twins were deaf, I immediately had a choice to make. Falling into despair would have given them fewer chances to develop. Taking bold action and following the advice from the doctors changed all of that. Today, I am amazed by what we achieved and by how much we have learned, and still learn every day.

There are many ways to find your rainbow in life. It's crucial to draw on the strength inside you. I teach my kids to focus on what they really want to be and what they want to do. I focus on their abilities, and I do that with adults too because not all of us have been given that foundation.

My kids need to learn how the world works, and not think that we live in a bubble. People say we are brave, but we had no choice. Both of us had a clear target which gave us the strength to always move on, even with problems. Even when Alessandro felt lost, he knew he had to find a solution, so he cycled. When you take care of yourself, love yourself, find yourself and your body, things change. The physical can have such an effect on the psychological.

Forget about what other people think of your child. If it's not a problem for you, it doesn't matter what they think. If you hide, you make it worse. It is horrible when people stare at your kids, but you need to move on. True drive always comes from authenticity and truth, and your children will blossom if you teach them that lesson. It can take only one person to speak the truth and that can start a flood. It's hard in the beginning to not care about what other people think and say about your child, but you must remember that your kids will feel there are problems if you do, or if you pass that over to them.

I got some things wrong, I won't deny that, but I hope others can learn from my mistakes. I didn't care about myself and I thought I had no time. I believed that if I took care of myself I'd be selfish, and I'd be seen as selfish. I also took absolutely no care of our relationship. We all need to remember that it is harder to repair a broken marriage than to put the work in at the time. I wish that I had only listened to experts, not to doom-mongers. I wish that I had never cared about judgemental people and only listened to the good ones. I wish that I had never measured me or my children against others. Kids remember you saying things that kill their spirit. The way you speak to your kids becomes their inner voice. Always give them love and support, and be kind enough to give that to yourself too.

When you have a problem, life still gives you more – you can't avoid further bad things happening just because you had some in the past. Without strategies, they will just pile up, so it would be madness to not develop those strategies as soon as you can. Schools don't really teach our children about mental health, so it is up to us parents to provide that whenever we can. From AVT we learned to be constant, to progress little by little every day to reach the goal. We can all take that message on board – life is about the small, incremental steps that lead you to your goal. Take the time to enjoy the journey as you get there as we only pass this way once. Like Jonathan Livingston, my children are flying – we're all flying.

Dylan recently said to me, 'We are a very strange family, Mummy!' I looked at him, his brother and his sister, and I laughed at this wise little person in front of me. Yes, we are strange, yes, we have battled to get here . . . but the wonderful thing is, that old man was right all those years ago.

Spring did come.

And it is wonderful.

La primavera arriva sempre ed e' bellissima.

EPILOGUE
LISTEN

There are truths given to us by our hearts and by our souls throughout our lives. All of us are given the opportunity to learn from those truths but we have to do one thing.

Listen.

Open your ears – take in all the world has to offer.

Listen.

If you trust in yourself, you will know what to do, what choices to make, what wars to fight.

Listen to everything the universe tells you. Your knowledge will be enriched beyond your wildest dreams if you can only see what there is when you take that leap. Embrace diversity, fight for what matters. Accept that not everyone is the same but cherish the fact that we can learn from each other, no matter what path we have each taken or what differences we may have.

The world is a wonderful tapestry and we are so lucky to be here, at this moment. How fortunate are we that we are living these lives at this time? Don't be afraid to speak your truth, to take on battles which might seem beyond your abilities at first, but which can become your greatest achievements.

We are a family who laughs and lives loudly. That way of being is in our very DNA. The thought that Dylan and Zack could have been excluded from that could break my heart, but I choose to concentrate on what we have achieved, what *they* have achieved. Don't look at what you have lost, and certainly don't dwell on what you *could* have lost.

Look at the possibilities and pay heed to the beat of your passion, which tells you what is right for you and for the ones you adore. We love for a reason and we have incredible depths that we can rely on for the people we walk beside on this journey.

Never lose hope – always remember that you can do this. You can do anything.

Just listen. Always listen.

LETTERS TO MY CHILDREN

To Keisha –

From the moment you arrived, you were the star of our lives. It was you who began our family and we will never forget that. The little girl with the huge hair and the big eyes, who never blinked, who never faltered as she watched us, as she took in everything about her new world. And that was how you stayed – always calm, never jealous, so helpful through all of those trips to hospital and through surgery for your little brothers.

Keisha, you did not come from my tummy, but you stole my heart. You were just the daughter I had been dreaming of, and you were just the daughter I needed. You always have the right answer and you never doubt that you can find a way. I have lost count of the number of times your little voice has said to me, 'Mummy, don't worry – I will find a solution.'

You are a strong girl who believes in herself and you will be a strong woman who believes in herself too. You face your challenges head on and overcome them with hard work and determination. Always be proud of this attitude for it is a wonderful thing. I hope it is something you have forever. There will be no mountain you cannot climb. I love you to the moon and back, Keisha – always be proud of who you are, where you came from, and your birth family.

You are so open-minded, so proud of your skin, of your past. You are caring and patient with your brothers, looking out for them, sharing and loving at all times. When that doctor said to me of my baby, 'I have never seen a girl so strong,' she could not have predicted how you would build on that. Your body and your mind will take you on an amazing journey, filled as they are with curiosity and strength. You will have an incredible life, Keisha, and I hope we have given you the foundations for that.

Love comes from what you build, love comes from a place deep inside. Every day I spend with you, I cherish the girl that you are and see the woman you will become. You have been a gift to us, Keisha, and I see our future together as a beautiful one. The first building brick of our family, our remarkable daughter.

To Dylan –

You are so fast in everything you want to do; you speed from one thing to the next, always wanting to know, always wanting to learn. You are such a competitive boy and I love that in you. You always focus on your abilities, Dylan, and I know that you always want to win – not to demonstrate to others how good you are, but to demonstrate to yourself. You immediately understand things and I hope you will always have that combination of a thirst for knowledge and a natural ability to comprehend it all. You have an obsession with geography and will travel the world. I know that because, like me, you want to see different cultures, meet different people and broaden your mind wherever you can. I know you will probably be the one to leave me first as you search for knowledge everywhere you can reach, but that will be fine. Your independence is another strength. I know you compare yourself to Zack a lot, but I would love for you to move on from that – you are you, and you are a very special boy who I love with all my heart.

To Zack –

You are such a funny boy! You make me laugh so much, Zack, and you are always laughing. Your reading is incredible, and you are very proud of your abilities in that, as you should be. I know that you are so clever but also that you revel in developing academic skills. All of your teachers know how intelligent you are, but the thing most people pick up on very quickly is that you are completely incapable of telling a lie. You are the most honest person I have ever met, and it is you who admits to everything when the three of you are being asked about what has happened. That face and that heart cannot lie. You are like an open book – so pure of heart and without any guile whatsoever. Always be as honest, that is what I wish for you.

You recently told me, 'I want to be a rock star. The music is in my mind and my body, Mum. I want a guitar and to travel around the world.' You will do it, you will do whatever you set your mind to as we have always said, 'Focus on your skills.' I believe that has seeped into every bone in your body, Zack, and that you believe, as I do, that we grow great through our dreams. They are what make us, they are what we work towards, and they will make you what you are destined to be.

You are such a great boy who will reach every one of your goals. You always want to know where I am, and when I will be there, but listen to this my darling son – even if I am not there with you, you can be independent. It is the love that I have given you which will ensure this happens. It flows through you and gives you the strength to be you. We will always protect you, and hopefully always be there to cuddle you as you love to be cuddled. You fill me with happiness, Zack, and I love the happy, funny, honest boy that we have made.

Finally, to Ale –

You are the best husband ever and I want to thank you with all my heart for encouraging me to write this book. You believed in me and that made me believe in myself despite all of this, for all the time. Thank you for being an incredible daddy for Keisha, Zack and Dylan, and thank you for being there for me. We made our family after all – and what a family it is!

ACKNOWLEDGMENTS

This book is my story. It is the story of my family and the way in which everyone can decide to face life head on and meet the difficulties they may encounter along the way with perseverance and commitment. It was a long journey and during the trip I met many professional and supportive people, with those who showed a human side to the process adding so much more than they could ever imagine. Each of them played a role in our experience, each of them inspired me and gave me a reason to smile. The journey was lengthy and I found hills, mountains, high waves, and ebbs and flows, but we always managed to face everything with the love and passion which has been the basis of our relationship since the beginning. We had to trust in our abilities and in those of our children - their incredible abilities.

I thank all of the NYU doctors who helped us to reach our goal quickly, and I thank them for the humanity they have always shown us along the way. Dr J. Thomas Roland and Dr Terri Shaw are two unique and outstanding doctors, who changed the lives of Dylan and Zack. Dr Janet E. Green always welcomed us with a smile which lifted us no matter what. Dr William H. Shapiro and his team provided so much assistance and support along the way.

I thank Lilian Flores for all she taught us, and Susannah Burden who is the best AVT ever! You have both been an inspiration and a guide for us; thanks to you, our children have wings to fly.

I thank AVUK for having always been there for us with the utmost professionalism.

I thank all our friends around the world who, with even just one word, have helped. Many of them are dear to us but, in particular, I would like to thank Claire Dutoit, Anna Burnat, Amparo Panya Nadal and her family, Marisa Sapena and her family, Annarita Scivales, and Yuisa Gonzales. You have been so important to me, Alessandro, and our children!

I thank Jodi Cutler who has been my inspiration and who has taught me that you can really make a change in someone's life, just by being you. She is an inspiration for me, not just as a mum but particularly as a woman.

A huge thanks to our families – to my mother, who has always given me positivity and self-confidence; to my sister and her family, who have always called me with assurance and without tears; to all the cousins, who have always welcomed my children and played with them without ever seeing differences; to my in-laws, who were exceptional at the beginning and continue to help us on everything and with great positivity.

I thank the school of Zack and Dylan and Keisha, Bathwick St Mary, especially Mr Kevin Purkiss and their teachers Mrs Claire Rigby and Mrs Allie Elliot. You are heroes for them, as well as great guides and a source of inspiration. Every child needs a hero and we are lucky to have so many of them!

I thank my daughter, Keisha, for always being so mature from the beginning and for having always loved her brothers without a limit. She is always proud of them and loves me and Ale to madness! Without you, my darling daughter, this would not have been possible.

Of course, I must thank my husband, Alessandro, for encouraging me to write this book and for the serenity that he always showed me even when things were so very difficult. He has always believed in us as a family and has always fought so hard to get us all the best care possible.

I thank Linda Watson-Brown for writing a book with me that I hope will inspire others around the world to always believe in their own possibilities and learn to listen. She is a writer of great moral and professional value.

I thank and dedicate this book to my father, Aldo, who has always believed in me. He has always encouraged me to be myself and today he would be happy and proud of me and of my children.

Thank you all. I hope that one day, when my children fulfil their wonderful promise, you will all see just what has been achieved through love and belief and dedication.

ABOUT THE AUTHOR

Born in sunny and windy Brindisi, on the heel of the Italian boot, Deborah Pezzuto moved to Florence for her University studies and later to Milan, where she started her career as a media and advertising executive.

She spent 20 years working in a highly demanding yet rewarding corporate environment, doing a job she loved and growing a great deal both personally and professionally.

Her life took a twist when she moved to New York City with her partner, Alessandro, and decided to start a family.

The adoption process of her daughter, Keisha, and the profound deafness of her twin sons, Zack and Dylan, profoundly changed how Deborah saw her life.

Knocked off her balance, Deborah had to significantly adapt her life and find within her the strength to give her children a chance to reach their full potential, despite their hearing disability, whilst raising Keisha in the most supportive environment possible.

Throughout this journey, she discovered inside her a force and a character that she had never imagined she had.

She subsequently developed the appetite to put her experience at the service of other women who are willing to find meaning and independence in their life, and families who are going through challenging times, especially those who are welcoming to this world children with special needs.

Today, Deborah is an established life coach, working with numerous clients around the world, collaborating with both individuals and corporations to develop their resilience and live a more fulfilled life.

She is the co-founder of 'AViTalia', a Facebook group to support families with children with hearing loss, and she is the administrator of 'Affrontiamo la Sordita' Insieme: Cochlear Implant Forum', the largest Facebook community in Italy to help families find useful resources to facilitate their Cochlear Implant journey.

If you would like to reach out to Deborah, you can contact her at deborah.pezzuto@gmail.com.

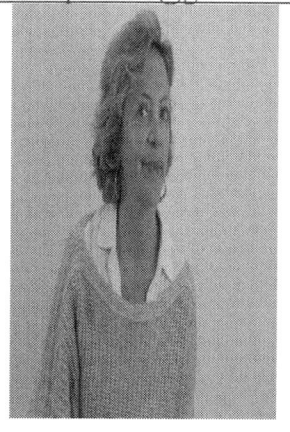

Printed in Great Britain
by Amazon